# WORD BY WORD

## Second Edition

## PICTURE DICTIONARY

### Steven J. Molinsky • Bill Bliss

Illustrated by
**Richard E. Hill**

PEARSON
Longman

Not for Sale in the U.S.

Dedicated to Janet Johnston in honor of her wonderful contribution
to the development of our textbooks over three decades.

*Steven J. Molinsky*
*Bill Bliss*

Word by Word Picture Dictionary, second edition

Pearson Education, 10 Bank Street, White Plains, NY 10606

Editorial director:  Pam Fishman
Vice president, director of design and production:  Rhea Banker
Director of electronic production:  Aliza Greenblatt
Director of manufacturing:  Patrice Fraccio
Senior manufacturing manager:  Edith Pullman
Marketing managers:  Vivian Shantz, Carol Brown
Senior digital layout specialist:  Wendy Wolf
Text design:  Wendy Wolf
Cover design:  Tracey Munz Cataldo
Realia creation:  Warren Fischbach, Paula Williams
Illustrations:  Richard E. Hill
Contributing artists:  Steven Young, Charles Cawley, Willard Gage, Marlon Violette

**ISBN 0-13-148218-1**
Longman on the Web
Longman.com offers online resources for teachers and students.  Access our Companion Websites, our online
catalog, and our local offices around the world.

Visit us at longman.com.

Printed in the United States of America
14 – V082 – 13 12

# CONTENTS

| Unit / Theme | Communication Skills | Writing & Discussion |
|---|---|---|
| **1** Personal Information and Family | • Asking for & giving personal information<br>• Identifying information on a form<br>• Spelling name aloud<br>• Identifying family members<br>• Introducing others | • Telling about yourself<br>• Telling about family members<br>• Drawing a family tree |
| **2** Common Everyday Activities and Language | • Identifying classroom objects & locations<br>• Identifying classroom actions<br>• Giving & following simple classroom commands<br>• Identifying everyday & leisure activities<br>• Inquiring by phone about a person's activities<br>• Asking about a person's plan for future activities<br>• Social communication: Greeting people, Leave taking, Introducing yourself & others, Getting someone's attention, Expressing gratitude, Saying you don't understand, Calling someone on the telephone<br>• Describing the weather<br>• Interpreting temperatures on a thermometer (Fahrenheit & Centigrade)<br>• Describing the weather forecast for tomorrow | • Describing a classroom<br>• Making a list of daily activities<br>• Describing daily routine<br>• Making a list of planned activities<br>• Describing favorite leisure activities<br>• Describing the weather |
| **3** Numbers/ Time/ Money/ Calendar | • Using cardinal & ordinal numbers<br>• Giving information about age, number of family members, residence<br>• Telling time<br>• Indicating time of events<br>• Asking for information about arrival & departure times<br>• Identifying coins & currency – names & values<br>• Making & asking for change<br>• Identifying days of the week<br>• Identifying months of the year<br>• Asking about the year, month, day, date<br>• Asking about the date of a birthday, anniversary, appointment<br>• Giving date of birth | • Describing numbers of students in a class<br>• Identifying a country's population<br>• Describing daily schedule with times<br>• Telling about time management<br>• Telling about the use of time in different cultures or countries<br>• Describing the cost of purchases<br>• Describing coins & currency of other countries<br>• Describing weekday & weekend activities<br>• Telling about favorite day of the week & month of the year |
| **4** Home | • Identifying types of housing & communities<br>• Requesting a taxi<br>• Calling 911 for an ambulance<br>• Identifying rooms of a home<br>• Identifying furniture<br>• Complimenting<br>• Asking for information in a store<br>• Locating items in a store<br>• Asking about items on sale<br>• Asking the location of items at home<br>• Telling about past weekend activities<br>• Identifying locations in an apartment building<br>• Identifying ways to look for housing: classified ads, listings, vacancy signs<br>• Renting an apartment<br>• Describing household problems<br>• Securing home repair services<br>• Making a suggestion<br>• Identifying household cleaning items, home supplies, & tools<br>• Asking to borrow an item<br>• Describing current home activities & plans for future activities | • Describing types of housing where people live<br>• Describing rooms & furniture in a residence<br>• Telling about baby products & early child-rearing practices in different countries<br>• Telling about personal experiences with repairing things<br>• Describing an apartment building<br>• Describing household cleaning chores |
| **5** Community | • Identifying places in the community<br>• Exchanging greetings<br>• Asking & giving the location of places in the community<br>• Identifying government buildings, services, & other places in a city/town center<br>• Identifying modes of transportation in a city/town center | • Describing places in a neighborhood<br>• Making a list of places, people, & actions observed at an intersection |

| Unit / Theme | Communication Skills | Writing & Discussion |
|---|---|---|
| **6** **Describing** | • Describing people by age<br>• Describing people by physical characteristics<br>• Describing a suspect or missing person to a police officer<br>• Describing people & things using adjectives<br>• Describing physical states & emotions<br>• Expressing concern about another person's physical state or emotion | • Describing physical characteristics of yourself & family members<br>• Describing physical characteristics of a favorite actor or actress or other famous person<br>• Describing things at home & in the community<br>• Telling about personal experiences with different emotions |
| **7** **Food** | • Identifying food items (fruits, vegetables, meat, poultry, seafood, dairy products, juices, beverages, deli, frozen foods, snack foods, groceries)<br>• Identifying non-food items purchased in a supermarket (e.g., household supplies, baby products, pet food)<br>• Determining food needs to make a shopping list<br>• Asking the location of items in a supermarket<br>• Identifying supermarket sections<br>• Requesting items at a service counter in a supermarket<br>• Identifying supermarket checkout area personnel & items<br>• Identifying food containers & quantities<br>• Identifying units of measure<br>• Asking for & giving recipe instructions<br>• Complimenting someone on a recipe<br>• Offering to help with food preparation<br>• Identifying food preparation actions<br>• Identifying kitchen utensils & cookware<br>• Asking to borrow an item<br>• Comprehending product advertising<br>• Ordering fast food items, coffee shop items, & sandwiches<br>• Indicating a shortage of supplies to a co-worker or supervisor<br>• Taking customers' orders at a food service counter<br>• Identifying restaurant objects, personnel, & actions<br>• Making & following requests at work<br>• Identifying & correctly positioning silverware & plates in a table setting<br>• Inquiring in person about restaurant job openings<br>• Ordering from a restaurant menu<br>• Taking customers' orders as a waiter or waitress in a restaurant | • Describing favorite & least favorite foods<br>• Describing foods in different countries<br>• Making a shopping list<br>• Describing places to shop for food<br>• Telling about differences between supermarkets & food stores in different countries<br>• Making a list of items in kitchen cabinets & the refrigerator<br>• Describing recycling practices<br>• Describing a favorite recipe using units of measure<br>• Telling about use of kitchen utensils & cookware<br>• Telling about experience with different types of restaurants<br>• Describing restaurants and menus in different countries<br>• Describing favorite foods ordered in restaurants |
| **8** **Colors and Clothing** | • Identifying colors<br>• Complimenting someone on clothing<br>• Identifying clothing items, including outerwear, sleepwear, underwear, exercise clothing, footwear, jewelry, & accessories<br>• Talking about appropriate clothing for different weather conditions<br>• Expressing clothing needs to a store salesperson<br>• Locating clothing items<br>• Inquiring about ownership of found clothing items<br>• Indicating loss of a clothing item<br>• Asking about sale prices in a clothing store<br>• Reporting theft of a clothing item to the police<br>• Stating preferences during clothing shopping<br>• Expressing problems with clothing & the need for alterations<br>• Identifying laundry objects & activities<br>• Locating laundry products in a store | • Describing the flags of different countries<br>• Telling about emotions associated with different colors<br>• Telling about clothing & colors you like to wear<br>• Describing clothing worn at different occasions (e.g., going to schools, parties, weddings)<br>• Telling about clothing worn in different weather conditions<br>• Telling about clothing worn during exercise activities<br>• Telling about footwear worn during different activities<br>• Describing the color, material, size, & pattern of favorite clothing items<br>• Comparing clothing fashions now & a long time ago<br>• Telling about who does laundry at home |

| Unit / Theme | Communication Skills | Writing & Discussion |
|---|---|---|
| **9** <br> **Shopping** | • Identifying departments & services in a department store <br> • Asking the location of items in a department store <br> • Asking to buy, return, exchange, try on, & pay for department store items <br> • Asking about regular & sales prices, discounts, & sales tax <br> • Interpreting a sales receipt <br> • Offering assistance to customers as a salesperson <br> • Expressing needs to a salesperson in a store <br> • Identifying electronics products, including video & audio equipment, telephones, cameras, & computers <br> • Identifying components of a computer & common computer software <br> • Complimenting someone about an item & inquiring where it was purchased <br> • Asking a salesperson for advice about different brands of a product <br> • Identifying common toys & other items in a toy store <br> • Asking for advice about an appropriate gift for a child | • Describing a department store <br> • Telling about stores that have sales <br> • Telling about an item purchased on sale <br> • Comparing different types & brands of video & audio equipment <br> • Describing telephones & cameras <br> • Describing personal use of a computer <br> • Sharing opinions about how computers have changed the world <br> • Telling about popular toys in different countries <br> • Telling about favorite childhood toys |
| **10** <br> **Community Services** | • Requesting bank services & transactions (e.g., deposit, withdrawal, cashing a check, obtaining traveler's checks, opening an account, applying for a loan, exchanging currency) <br> • Identifying bank personnel <br> • Identifying bank forms <br> • Asking about acceptable forms of payment (cash, check, credit card, money order, traveler's check) <br> • Identifying household bills (rent, utilities, etc.) <br> • Identifying family finance documents & actions <br> • Following instructions to use an ATM machine <br> • Requesting post office services & transactions <br> • Identifying types of mail & mail services <br> • Identifying different ways to buy stamps <br> • Requesting non-mail services available at the post office (money order, selective service registration, passport application) <br> • Identifying & locating library sections, services, & personnel <br> • Asking how to find a book in the library <br> • Identifying community institutions, services, and personnel (police, fire, city government, public works, recreation, sanitation, religious institutions) <br> • Identifying types of emergency vehicles <br> • Reporting a crime <br> • Identifying community mishaps (gas leak, water main break, etc.) <br> • Expressing concern about community problems | • Describing use of bank services <br> • Telling about household bills & amounts paid <br> • Telling about the person responsible for household finances <br> • Describing use of ATM machines <br> • Describing use of postal services <br> • Comparing postal systems in different countries <br> • Telling about experience using a library <br> • Telling about the location of community institutions <br> • Describing experiences using community institutions <br> • Telling about crime in the community <br> • Describing experience with a crime or emergency |
| **11** <br> **Health** | • Identifying parts of the body & key internal organs <br> • Describing ailments, symptoms, & injuries <br> • Asking about the health of another person <br> • Identifying items in a first-aid kit <br> • Describing medical emergencies <br> • Identifying emergency medical procedures (CPR, rescue breathing, Heimlich maneuver) <br> • Calling 911 to report a medical emergency <br> • Identifying major illnesses <br> • Talking with a friend or co-worker about illness in one's family <br> • Following instructions during a medical examination <br> • Identifying medical personnel, equipment, & supplies in medical & dental offices <br> • Understanding medical & dental personnel's description of procedures during treatment <br> • Understanding a doctor's medical advice and instructions <br> • Identifying over-the-counter medications <br> • Understanding dosage instructions on medicine labels <br> • Identifying medical specialists <br> • Indicating the date & time of a medical appointment <br> • Identifying hospital departments & personnel <br> • Identifying equipment in a hospital room <br> • Identifying actions & items related to personal hygiene <br> • Locating personal care products in a store <br> • Identifying actions & items related to baby care | • Describing self <br> • Telling about a personal experience with an illness or injury <br> • Describing remedies or treatments for common problems (cold, stomachache, insect bite, hiccups) <br> • Describing experience with a medical emergency <br> • Describing a medical examination <br> • Describing experience with a medical or dental procedure <br> • Telling about medical advice received <br> • Telling about over-the-counter medications used <br> • Comparing use of medications in different countries <br> • Describing experience with a medical specialist <br> • Describing a hospital stay <br> • Making a list of personal care items needed for a trip <br> • Comparing baby products in different countries |

| Unit / Theme | Communication Skills | Writing & Discussion |
|---|---|---|
| **12** <br> School, Subjects, and Activities | • Identifying types of educational institutions <br> • Giving information about previous education during a job interview <br> • Identifying school locations & personnel <br> • Identifying school subjects <br> • Identifying extracurricular activities <br> • Sharing after-school plans <br> • MATH: <br>  • Asking & answering basic questions during a math class <br>  • Using fractions to indicate sale prices <br>  • Using percents to indicate test scores & probability in weather forecasts <br>  • Identifying high school math subjects <br>  • Using measurement terms to indicate height, width, depth, length, distance <br>  • Interpreting metric measurements <br>  • Identifying types of lines, geometric shapes, & solid figures <br> • ENGLISH LANGUAGE ARTS: <br>  • Identifying types of sentences <br>  • Identifying parts of speech <br>  • Identifying punctuation marks <br>  • Providing feedback during peer-editing <br>  • Identifying steps of the writing process <br>  • Identifying types of literature <br>  • Identifying forms of writing <br> • GEOGRAPHY: <br>  • Identifying geographical features & bodies of water <br>  • Identifying natural environments (desert, jungle, rainforest, etc.) <br> • SCIENCE: <br>  • Identifying science classroom/laboratory equipment <br>  • Asking about equipment needed to do a science procedure <br>  • Identifying steps of the scientific method <br>  • Identifying key terms to describe the universe, solar system, & space exploration | • Telling about different types of schools in the community <br> • Telling about schools attended, where, when, & subjects studied <br> • Describing a school <br> • Comparing schools in different countries <br> • Telling about favorite school subject <br> • Telling about extracurricular activities <br> • Comparing extracurricular activities in different countries <br> • Describing math education <br> • Telling about something bought on sale <br> • Researching & sharing information about population statistics using percents <br> • Describing favorite books & authors <br> • Describing newspapers & magazines read <br> • Telling about use of different types of written communication <br> • Describing the geography of your country <br> • Describing geographical features experienced <br> • Describing experience with scientific equipment <br> • Describing science education <br> • Brainstorming a science experiment & describing each step of the scientific method <br> • Drawing & naming a constellation <br> • Expressing an opinion about the importance of space exploration |
| **13** <br> Work | • Identifying occupations <br> • Stating work experience (including length of time in an occupation) during a job interview <br> • Talking about occupation during social conversation <br> • Expressing job aspirations <br> • Identifying job skills & work activities <br> • Indicating job skills during an interview (including length of time) <br> • Identifying types of job advertisements (help wanted signs, job notices, classified ads) <br> • Interpreting abbreviations in job advertisements <br> • Identifying each step in a job-search process <br> • Identifying workplace locations, furniture, equipment, & personnel <br> • Identifying common office tasks <br> • Asking the location of a co-worker <br> • Engaging in small-talk with co-workers <br> • Identifying common office supplies <br> • Making requests at work <br> • Repeating to confirm understanding of a request or instruction <br> • Identifying factory locations, equipment, & personnel <br> • Asking the location of workplace departments & personnel to orient oneself as a new employee <br> • Asking about the location & activities of a co-worker <br> • Identifying construction site machinery, equipment, and building materials <br> • Asking a co-worker for a workplace item <br> • Warning a co-worker of a safety hazard <br> • Asking whether there is a sufficient supply of workplace materials <br> • Identifying job safety equipment <br> • Interpreting warning signs at work <br> • Reminding someone to use safety equipment <br> • Asking the location of emergency equipment at work | • Career exploration: sharing ideas about occupations that are interesting, difficult <br> • Describing occupation & occupations of family members <br> • Describing job skills <br> • Describing a familiar job (skill requirements, qualifications, hours, salary) <br> • Telling about how people found their jobs <br> • Telling about experience with a job search or job interview <br> • Describing a familiar workplace <br> • Telling about office & school supplies used <br> • Describing a nearby factory & working conditions there <br> • Comparing products produced by factories in different countries <br> • Describing building materials used in ones dwelling <br> • Describing a nearby construction site <br> • Telling about experience with safety equipment <br> • Describing the use of safety equipment in the community |

| Unit / Theme | Communication Skills | Writing & Discussion |
|---|---|---|
| **14** <br> **Transportation and Travel** | • Identifying modes of local & inter-city public transportation <br> • Expressing intended mode of travel <br> • Asking about a location to obtain transportation (bus stop, bus station, train station, subway station) <br> • Locating ticket counters, information booths, fare card machines, & information signage in transportation stations <br> • Identifying types of vehicles <br> • Indicating to a car salesperson need for a type of vehicle <br> • Describing a car accident <br> • Identifying parts of a car & maintenance items <br> • Indicating a problem with a car <br> • Requesting service or assistance at a service station <br> • Identifying types of highway lanes & markings, road structures (tunnels, bridges, etc.), traffic signage, & local intersection road markings <br> • Reporting the location of an accident <br> • Giving & following driving directions (using prepositions of motion) <br> • Interpreting traffic signs <br> • Warning a driver about an upcoming sign <br> • Interpreting compass directions <br> • Asking for driving directions <br> • Following instructions during a driver's test <br> • Repeating to confirm instructions <br> • Identifying airport locations & personnel (check-in, security, gate, baggage claim, Customs & Immigration) <br> • Asking for location of places & personnel at an airport <br> • Indicating loss of travel documents or other items <br> • Identifying airplane sections, seating areas, emergency equipment, & flight personnel <br> • Identifying steps in the process of airplane travel (actions in the security area, at the gate, boarding, & being seated) <br> • Following instructions of airport security personnel, gate attendants, & flight crew <br> • Identifying sections of a hotel & personnel <br> • Asking for location of places & personnel in a hotel | • Describing mode of travel to different places in the community <br> • Describing local public transportation <br> • Comparing transportation in different countries <br> • Telling about common types of vehicles in different countries <br> • Expressing opinion about favorite type of vehicle & manufacturer <br> • Expressing opinion about most important features to look for when making a car purchase <br> • Describing experience with car repairs <br> • Describing a local highway <br> • Describing a local intersection <br> • Telling about dangerous traffic areas where many accidents occur <br> • Describing your route from home to school <br> • Describing how to get to different places from home and school <br> • Describing local traffic signs <br> • Comparing traffic signs in different countries <br> • Describing a familiar airport <br> • Telling about an experience with Customs & Immigration <br> • Describing an air travel experience <br> • Using imagination: being an airport security officer giving passengers instructions; being a flight attendant giving passengers instructions before take-off <br> • Describing a familiar hotel <br> • Expressing opinion about hotel jobs that are most interesting, most difficult |
| **15** <br> **Recreation and Entertainment** | • Identifying common hobbies, crafts, & games & related materials/equipment <br> • Describing favorite leisure activities <br> • Purchasing craft supplies, equipment, & other products in a store <br> • Asking for & offering a suggestion for a leisure activity <br> • Identifying places to go for outdoor recreation, entertainment, culture, etc. <br> • Describing past weekend activities <br> • Describing activities planned for a future day off or weekend <br> • Identifying features & equipment in a park & playground <br> • Asking the location of a park feature or equipment <br> • Warning a child to be careful on playground equipment <br> • Identifying features of a beach, common beach items, & personnel <br> • Identifying indoor & outdoor recreation activities & sports, & related equipment & supplies <br> • Asking if someone remembered an item when preparing for an activity <br> • Identifying team sports & terms for players, playing fields, & equipment <br> • Commenting on a player's performance during a game <br> • Indicating that you can't find an item <br> • Asking the location of sports equipment in a store <br> • Reminding someone of items needed for a sports activity <br> • Identifying types of winter/water sports, recreation, & equipment <br> • Engaging in small talk about favorite sports & recreation activities <br> • Using the telephone to inquire whether a store sells a product <br> • Making & responding to an invitation <br> • Following a teacher or coach's instructions during sports practice, P.E. class, & an exercise class <br> • Identifying types of entertainment & cultural events, & the performers <br> • Commenting on a performance <br> • Identifying genres of music, plays, movies, & TV programs <br> • Expressing likes about types of entertainment <br> • Identifying musical instruments <br> • Complimenting someone on musical ability | • Describing a favorite hobby, craft, or game <br> • Comparing popular games in different countries, and how to play them <br> • Describing favorite places to go & activities there <br> • Describing a local park & playground <br> • Describing a favorite beach & items used there <br> • Describing an outdoor recreation experience <br> • Describing favorite individual sports & recreation activities <br> • Describing favorite team sports & famous players <br> • Comparing popular sports in different countries <br> • Describing experience with winter or water sports & recreation <br> • Expressing opinions about Winter Olympics sports (most exciting, most dangerous) <br> • Describing exercise habits & routines <br> • Using imagination: being an exercise instructor leading a class <br> • Telling about favorite types of entertainment <br> • Comparing types of entertainment popular in different countries <br> • Telling about favorite performers <br> • Telling about favorite types of music, movies, & TV programs <br> • Describing experience with a musical instrument <br> • Comparing typical musical instruments in different countries |

| Unit / Theme | Communication Skills | Writing & Discussion |
|---|---|---|
| **16** **Nature** | • Identifying places & people on a farm<br>• Identifying farm animals & crops<br>• Identifying animals & pets<br>• Identifying birds & insects<br>• Identifying fish, sea animals, amphibians, & reptiles<br>• Asking about the presence of wildlife in an area<br>• Identifying trees, plants, & flowers<br>• Identifying key parts of a tree and flower<br>• Asking for information about trees & flowers<br>• Warning someone about poisonous vegetation in an area<br>• Identifying sources of energy<br>• Describing the kind of energy used to heat homes & for cooking<br>• Expressing an opinion about good future sources of energy<br>• Identifying behaviors that promote conservation (recycling, conserving energy, conserving water, carpooling)<br>• Expressing concern about environmental problems<br>• Identifying different kinds of natural disasters | • Comparing farms in different countries<br>• Telling about local animals, animals in a zoo, & common local birds & insects<br>• Comparing common pets in different countries<br>• Using imagination: what animal you would like to be, & why<br>• Telling a popular folk tale or children's story about animals, birds, or insects<br>• Describing fish, sea animals, & reptiles in different countries<br>• Identifying endangered species<br>• Expressing opinions about wildlife – most interesting, beautiful, dangerous<br>• Describing local trees & flowers, & favorites<br>• Comparing different cultures' use of flowers at weddings, funerals, holidays, & hospitals<br>• Expressing an opinion about an environmental problem<br>• Telling about how people prepare for natural disasters |
| **17** **International Travel and Tourism** | • TYPES OF TRAVEL:<br>  • Identifying types of travel (business & family trips, tours, modes of travel)<br>  • Identifying ways to book a trip<br>  • Talking about travel plans<br>• ARRIVING AT A DESTINATION:<br>  • Locating airport services upon arrival at a destination<br>  • Identifying travel documents (passport, visa, baggage claim check, customs declaration form)<br>  • Producing travel documents when requested by airport personnel<br>  • Passing through immigration/passport control: explaining the purpose of a trip (business/pleasure) and length of stay<br>  • Passing through customs: responding to questions and requests of customs official (stating number of bags; opening bags when requested)<br>• HOTEL COMMUNICATION:<br>  • Identifying different types of hotel rooms<br>  • Checking in/Requesting a room<br>  • Using a room telephone to request hotel services<br>  • Ordering food from room service<br>  • Calling housekeeping to request room supplies<br>  • Calling to report a maintenance problem in a room<br>  • Requesting a wake-up call<br>  • Calling the concierge to make a request<br>  • Calling the bell desk to request assistance checking out<br>• TOURIST ACTIVITIES:<br>  • Identifying common tourist activities (sightseeing, tours, exchanging money, buying souvenirs, making reservations, renting a car, getting tickets, shopping, visiting local attractions)<br>  • Expressing tourist activity interests to a hotel concierge<br>  • Reporting about tourist activities<br>• TOURIST COMMUNICATION:<br>  • Making requests (to exchange money, cash traveler's checks, purchase something, buy tickets, mail something)<br>  • Inquiring about permissibility (to take photographs, eat, enter, use a cell phone, or use a credit card in various locations)<br>  • Talking with local people (about where you are from, length of your stay, what you have seen, and your opinion of their city)<br>  • Using emergency expressions (to call for help, to call for the police, to avoid someone who is bothering you)<br>  • Understanding emergency expressions (about a fire, about an imminent hazard)<br>  • Understanding a police command to stop (Freeze! Stop! Don't move!)<br>  • Asking someone if they speak your language<br>  • Asking someone to write down an address or other information<br>  • Asking what an object is called in English while pointing to it<br>  • Asking for repetition & clarification<br>  • Asking someone to speak slowly | • Telling about a trip (location, kind of trip, how it was arranged)<br>• Telling about arrival at a destination<br>• Telling about an experience staying in a hotel, including type of room and hotel services used<br>• Telling about tourism experiences |

*Welcome to the second edition of the* WORD BY WORD *Picture Dictionary!* This text presents more than 4,000 vocabulary words through vibrant illustrations and simple accessible lesson pages that are designed for clarity and ease-of-use with learners at all levels. Our goal is to help students practice English used in everyday life, in the community, in school, at work, and in international travel.

WORD BY WORD organizes the vocabulary into 17 thematic units, providing a careful research-based sequence of lessons that integrates students' development of grammar and vocabulary skills through topics that begin with the immediate world of the student and progress to the world at large. Early lessons on the family, the home, and daily activities lead to lessons on the community, school, workplace, shopping, recreation, and other topics. In addition to developing students' vocabulary, the text also serves as a comprehensive communication skills program that integrates vocabulary learning, listening and speaking skills, and themes for writing and discussion. The Scope & Sequence on the previous pages illustrates the unique curriculum and skills integration in the program.

Since each lesson in *Word by Word* is self-contained, it can be used either sequentially or in any desired order. For users' convenience, the lessons are listed in two ways: sequentially in the Table of Contents, and alphabetically in the Thematic Index. These resources, combined with the Glossary in the appendix, allow students and teachers to quickly and easily locate all words and topics in the Picture Dictionary.

The *Word by Word* Picture Dictionary is the centerpiece of the complete *Word by Word* Vocabulary Development Program, which offers a wide selection of print and media support materials for instruction at all levels.

Workbooks at different levels offer flexible options to meet students' needs. Vocabulary Workbooks at Beginning and Intermediate levels feature motivating vocabulary, grammar, and listening practice. A Literacy Workbook provides all-skills practice especially appropriate for learners who are not familiar with the alphabet or who need a pre-Beginning-level introduction to English vocabulary, reading, and writing.

The Teacher's Guide and Lesson Planner with CD-ROM includes lesson-planning suggestions, community tasks, Internet weblinks, and reproducible masters to save teachers hours of lesson preparation time. An Activity Handbook with step-by-step teaching strategies for key vocabulary development activities is included in the Teacher's Guide.

The Audio Program includes all words and conversations for interactive practice and —as bonus material—an expanded selection of WordSongs for entertaining musical practice with the vocabulary.

Additional ancillary materials include Color Transparencies, Vocabulary Game Cards, a Testing Program, and ExamView CD-ROM. Bilingual Editions are also available.

## Teaching Strategies

*Word by Word* presents vocabulary words in context. Model conversations depict situations in which people use the words in meaningful communication. These models become the basis for students to engage in dynamic, interactive practice. In addition, writing and discussion questions in each lesson encourage students to relate the vocabulary and themes to their own lives as they share experiences, thoughts, opinions, and information about themselves, their cultures, and their countries. In this way, students get to know each other "word by word."

In using *Word by Word*, we encourage you to develop approaches and strategies that are compatible with your own teaching style and the needs and abilities of your students. You may find it helpful to incorporate some of the following techniques for presenting and practicing the vocabulary in each lesson.

1. **Preview the Vocabulary:** Activate students' prior knowledge of the vocabulary by brainstorming with students the words in the lesson they already know and writing them on the board, or by having students look at the transparency or the illustration in *Word by Word* and identify the words they are familiar with.

2. **Present the Vocabulary:** Using the transparency or the illustration in the Picture Dictionary, point to the picture of each word, say the word, and have the class repeat it chorally and individually. (You can also play the word list on the Audio Program.) Check students' understanding and pronunciation of the vocabulary.

3. **Vocabulary Practice:** Have students practice the vocabulary as a class, in pairs, or in small groups. Say or write a word, and have students point to the item or tell the number. Or, point to an item or give the number, and have students say the word.

4. **Model Conversation Practice:** Some lessons have model conversations that use the first word in the vocabulary list. Other models are in the form of skeletal dialogs, in which vocabulary words can be inserted. (In many skeletal dialogs, bracketed numbers indicate which words can be used for practicing the conversation. If no bracketed numbers appear, all the words in the lesson can be used.)

   The following steps are recommended for Model Conversation Practice:

   a. Preview: Have students look at the model illustration and discuss who they think the speakers are and where the conversation takes place.

   b. The teacher presents the model or plays the audio one or more times and checks students' understanding of the situation and the vocabulary.

   c. Students repeat each line of the conversation chorally and individually.

   d. Students practice the model in pairs.

   e. A pair of students presents a conversation based on the model, but using a different word from the vocabulary list.

   f. In pairs, students practice several conversations based on the model, using different words on the page.

   g. Pairs present their conversations to the class.

5. **Additional Conversation Practice:** Many lessons provide two additional skeletal dialogs for further conversation practice with the vocabulary. (These can be found in the yellow-shaded area at the bottom of the page.) Have students practice and present these conversations using any words they wish. Before they practice the additional conversations, you may want to have students listen to the sample additional conversations on the Audio Program.

6. **Spelling Practice:** Have students practice spelling the words as a class, in pairs, or in small groups. Say a word, and have students spell it aloud or write it. Or, using the transparency, point to an item and have students write the word.

7. **Themes for Discussion, Composition, Journals, and Portfolios:** Each lesson of *Word by Word* provides one or more questions for discussion and composition. (These can be found in a blue-shaded area at the bottom of the page.) Have students respond to the questions as a class, in pairs, or in small groups. Or, have students write their responses at home, share their written work with other students, and discuss as a class, in pairs, or in small groups.

   Students may enjoy keeping a journal of their written work. If time permits, you may want to write a response in each student's journal, sharing your own opinions and experiences as well as reacting to what the student has written. If you are keeping portfolios of students' work, these compositions serve as excellent examples of students' progress in learning English.

8. **Communication Activities:** The *Word by Word* Teacher's Guide and Lesson Planner with CD-ROM provides a wealth of games, tasks, brainstorming, discussion, movement, drawing, miming, role-playing, and other activities designed to take advantage of students' different learning styles and particular abilities and strengths. For each lesson, choose one or more of these activities to reinforce students' vocabulary learning in a way that is stimulating, creative, and enjoyable.

---

**WORD BY WORD** aims to offer students a communicative, meaningful, and lively way of practicing English vocabulary. In conveying to you the substance of our program, we hope that we have also conveyed the spirit: that learning vocabulary can be genuinely interactive . . . relevant to our students' lives . . . responsive to students' differing strengths and learning styles . . . and fun!

*Steven J. Molinsky*

*Bill Bliss*

**Registration Form**

| Name | Gloria | P. | Sanchez |
|---|---|---|---|
| | First | Middle Initial | Last |

| Address | 95 | Garden Street | 3G |
|---|---|---|---|
| | Number | Street | Apartment Number |
| | Los Angeles | CA | 90036 |
| | City | State | Zip Code |

Telephone __323-524-3278__   Cell Phone __323-695-1864__

E-Mail Address __gloria97@ail.com__   SSN __227-93-6185__   Sex M__ F **X**

Date of Birth __5/12/88__   Place of Birth __Centerville, Texas__

1 name
2 first name
3 middle initial
4 last name / family name / surname
5 address

6 street number
7 street
8 apartment number
9 city
10 state
11 zip code

12 area code
13 telephone number / phone number
14 cell phone number
15 e-mail address
16 social security number

17 sex
18 date of birth
19 place of birth

A. What's your **name**?
B. Gloria P. Sanchez.

A. What's your _____?
B. ..............
A. Did you say ..............?
B. Yes. That's right.

A. What's your last name?
B. ..............
A. How do you spell that?
B. ..............

Tell about yourself:
My name is ..............
My address is ..............
My telephone number is ..............

Now interview a friend.

| **1** husband | **children** | **siblings** | **grandparents** | **grandchildren** |
| **2** wife | **5** daughter | **8** sister | **10** grandmother | **12** granddaughter |
| | **6** son | **9** brother | **11** grandfather | **13** grandson |
| **parents** | **7** baby | | | |
| **3** father | | | | |
| **4** mother | | | | |

A. Who is he?
B. He's my **husband**.
A. What's his name?
B. His name is *Jack*.

A. Who is she?
B. She's my **wife**.
A. What's her name?
B. Her name is *Nancy*.

A. I'd like to introduce my _____.
B. Nice to meet you.
C. Nice to meet you, too.

A. What's your _____'s name?
B. His/Her name is ..............

Who are the people in your family?
What are their names?

Tell about photos of family members.

Helen  Walter

Jack  Nancy  Frank  Linda

Jennifer  Timmy  Alan

1 uncle
2 aunt
3 niece
4 nephew
5 cousin

6 mother-in-law
7 father-in-law
8 son-in-law
9 daughter-in-law
10 brother-in-law
11 sister-in-law

① Jack is Alan's ____.
② Nancy is Alan's ____.
③ Jennifer is Frank and Linda's ____.
④ Timmy is Frank and Linda's ____.
⑤ Alan is Jennifer and Timmy's ____.

⑥ Helen is Jack's ____.
⑦ Walter is Jack's ____.
⑧ Jack is Helen and Walter's ____.
⑨ Linda is Helen and Walter's ____.
⑩ Frank is Jack's ____.
⑪ Linda is Jack's ____.

A. Who is he/she?
B. He's/She's my _____.
A. What's his/her name?
B. His/Her name is _____.

A. Let me introduce my _____.
B. I'm glad to meet you.
C. Nice meeting you, too.

Tell about your relatives:
   What are their names?
   Where do they live?

Draw your family tree and tell about it.

1 teacher
2 teacher's aide
3 student
4 desk
5 seat/chair
6 table
7 computer
8 overhead projector
9 screen
10 chalkboard/board
11 clock
12 map
13 bulletin board
14 P.A. system/
   loudspeaker
15 whiteboard/board
16 globe
17 bookcase/bookshelf
18 teacher's desk
19 wastebasket

| | | | | |
|---|---|---|---|---|
| **20** pen | **24** book/textbook | **28** notebook paper | **32** chalk | **36** keyboard |
| **21** pencil | **25** workbook | **29** graph paper | **33** eraser | **37** monitor |
| **22** eraser | **26** spiral notebook | **30** ruler | **34** marker | **38** mouse |
| **23** pencil sharpener | **27** binder/notebook | **31** calculator | **35** thumbtack | **39** printer |

A. Where's the **teacher**?
B. The **teacher** is *next to* the **board**.

A. Where's the **globe**?
B. The **globe** is *on* the **bookcase**.

A. Is there a/an _____ in your classroom?*
B. Yes. There's a/an _____
   next to/on the _____.

A. Is there a/an _____ in your classroom?*
B. No, there isn't.

Describe your classroom.
(There's a/an .............)

* With 28, 29, 32 use: Is there _____ in your classroom?

| | | |
|---|---|---|
| 1 Say your name. | 11 Open your book. | 21 Do your homework. |
| 2 Repeat your name. | 12 Read page ten. | 22 Bring in your homework. |
| 3 Spell your name. | 13 Study page ten. | 23 Go over the answers. |
| 4 Print your name. | 14 Close your book. | 24 Correct your mistakes. |
| 5 Sign your name. | 15 Put away your book. | 25 Hand in your homework. |
| 6 Stand up. | 16 Raise your hand. | 26 Share a book. |
| 7 Go to the board. | 17 Ask a question. | 27 Discuss the question. |
| 8 Write on the board. | 18 Listen to the question. | 28 Help each other. |
| 9 Erase the board. | 19 Answer the question. | 29 Work together. |
| 10 Sit down. / Take your seat. | 20 Listen to the answer. | 30 Share with the class. |

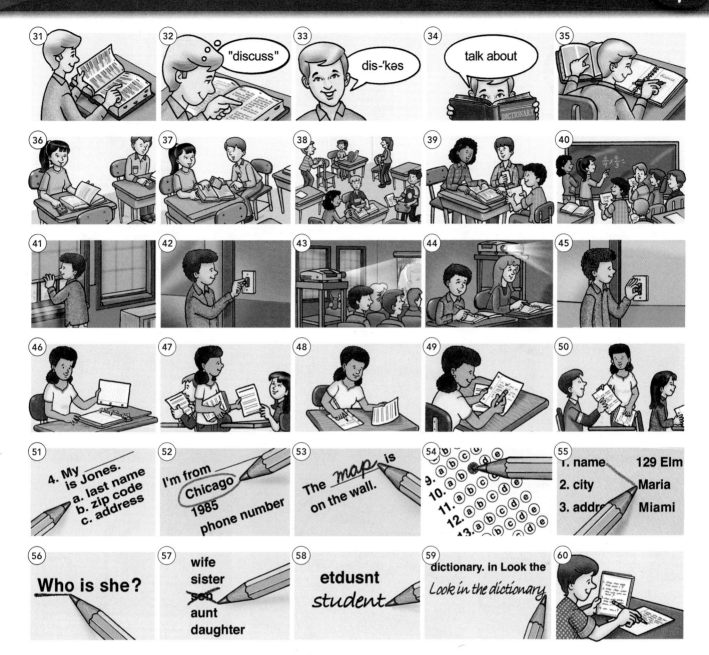

31 Look in the dictionary.
32 Look up a word.
33 Pronounce the word.
34 Read the definition.
35 Copy the word.

36 Work alone./Do your own work.
37 Work with a partner.
38 Break up into small groups.
39 Work in a group.
40 Work as a class.

41 Lower the shades.
42 Turn off the lights.
43 Look at the screen.
44 Take notes.
45 Turn on the lights.

46 Take out a piece of paper.
47 Pass out the tests.
48 Answer the questions.
49 Check your answers.
50 Collect the tests.

51 Choose the correct answer.
52 Circle the correct answer.
53 Fill in the blank.
54 Mark the answer sheet./
   Bubble the answer.
55 Match the words.

56 Underline the word.
57 Cross out the word.
58 Unscramble the word.
59 Put the words in order.
60 Write on a separate
   sheet of paper.

You're the teacher!
Give instructions to your students!

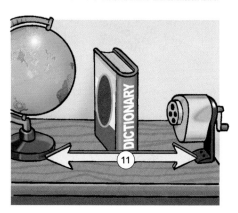

| | | | |
|---|---|---|---|
| 1 above | 5 next to | 8 to the left of | 10 in |
| 2 below | | 9 to the right of | |
| | 6 on | | 11 between |
| 3 in front of | 7 under | | |
| 4 behind | | | |

[1–10]
A. Where's the *clock*?
B. The *clock* is **above** the *bulletin board*.

[11]
A. Where's the *dictionary*?
B. The *dictionary* is **between** the *globe* and the *pencil sharpener*.

Tell about the classroom on page 4. Use the prepositions in this lesson.

Tell about your classroom.

1 get up
2 take a shower
3 brush *my** teeth
4 shave
5 get dressed

6 wash *my** face
7 put on makeup
8 brush *my** hair
9 comb *my** hair
10 make the bed

* my, his, her, our, your, their

11 get undressed
12 take a bath
13 go to bed
14 sleep

15 make breakfast
16 make lunch
17 cook / make dinner
18 eat / have breakfast
19 eat / have lunch
20 eat / have dinner

A. What do you do every day?
B. I **get up**, I **take a shower**, and I **brush my teeth**.

A. What does he do every day?
B. He _____s, he _____s, and he _____s.

A. What does she do every day?
B. She _____s, she _____s, and she_____s.

What do you do every day? Make a list.

Interview some friends and tell about their everyday activities.

1 clean the apartment/
   clean the house
2 wash the dishes
3 do the laundry
4 iron

5 feed the baby
6 feed the cat
7 walk the dog
8 study

9 go to work
10 go to school
11 drive to work
12 take the bus to school

13 work
14 leave work
15 go to the store
16 come home/get home

A. Hello. What are you doing?
B. I'm **clean**ing the **apartment**.

A. Hello, .............. This is ..............
   What are you doing?
B. I'm _____ing. How about you?
A. I'm _____ing.

A. Are you going to _____ soon?
B. Yes. I'm going to _____ in a
   little while.

What are you going to do tomorrow?
Make a list of everything you are
going to do.

1　watch TV
2　listen to the radio
3　listen to music
4　read a book

5　read the newspaper
6　play
7　play cards
8　play basketball

9　play the guitar
10　practice the piano
11　exercise
12　swim

13　plant flowers
14　use the computer
15　write a letter
16　relax

A.　Hi.　What are you doing?
B.　I'm **watch**ing **TV**.

A.　Hi, .............　Are you
　　_____ing?
B.　No, I'm not.　I'm _____ing.

A.　What's your (husband/wife/son/
　　daughter/. . .) doing?
B.　He's/She's _____ing.

What leisure activities do you like to do?

What do your family members and
friends like to do?

## Greeting People

## Leave Taking

1 Hello. / Hi.
2 Good morning.
3 Good afternoon.
4 Good evening.

5 How are you? / How are you doing?
6 Fine. / Fine, thanks. / Okay.
7 What's new? / What's new with you?
8 Not much. / Not too much.

9 Good-bye. / Bye.
10 Good night.
11 See you later. /
See you soon.

## Introducing Yourself and Others

## Getting Someone's Attention

## Expressing Gratitude

## Saying You Don't Understand

## Calling Someone on the Telephone

12 Hello. My name is ........./
Hi. I'm .........

13 Nice to meet you.

14 Nice to meet you, too.

15 I'd like to introduce ........./
This is .........

16 Excuse me.

17 May I ask a question?

18 Thank you. / Thanks.

19 You're welcome.

20 I don't understand. /
Sorry. I don't understand.

21 Can you please repeat that? /
Can you please say that again?

22 Hello. This is ......... May I please
speak to .........?

23 Yes. Hold on a moment.

24 I'm sorry. ......... isn't here right now.

Practice conversations with other students. Use all the expressions on pages 12 and 13.

## Weather

| | | |
|---|---|---|
| 1 sunny | 7 windy | 13 sleeting |
| 2 cloudy | 8 humid/muggy | 14 lightning |
| 3 clear | 9 raining | 15 thunderstorm |
| 4 hazy | 10 drizzling | 16 snowstorm |
| 5 foggy | 11 snowing | 17 dust storm |
| 6 smoggy | 12 hailing | 18 heat wave |

## Temperature

19 thermometer
20 Fahrenheit
21 Centigrade/Celsius
22 hot
23 warm
24 cool
25 cold
26 freezing

[1–13]
A.  What's the weather like?
B.  It's _____ .

[14–18]
A.  What's the weather forecast?
B.  There's going to be ___[14]___ /
     a ___[15–18]___ .

[20–26]
A.  How's the weather?
B.  It's ___[22–26]___ .
A.  What's the temperature?
B.  It's . . . degrees ___[20–21]___ .

What's the weather like today?  What's the temperature?

What's the weather forecast for tomorrow?

## Cardinal Numbers

| | | | |
|---|---|---|---|
| **0** zero | **11** eleven | **21** twenty-one | **101** one hundred (and) one |
| **1** one | **12** twelve | **22** twenty-two | **102** one hundred (and) two |
| **2** two | **13** thirteen | **30** thirty | **1,000** one thousand |
| **3** three | **14** fourteen | **40** forty | **10,000** ten thousand |
| **4** four | **15** fifteen | **50** fifty | **100,000** one hundred thousand |
| **5** five | **16** sixteen | **60** sixty | **1,000,000** one million |
| **6** six | **17** seventeen | **70** seventy | **1,000,000,000** one billion |
| **7** seven | **18** eighteen | **80** eighty | |
| **8** eight | **19** nineteen | **90** ninety | |
| **9** nine | **20** twenty | **100** one hundred | |
| **10** ten | | | |

A. How old are you?
B. I'm _____ years old.

A. How many people are there in your family?
B. _____.

## Ordinal Numbers

| | | | |
|---|---|---|---|
| **1st** first | **11th** eleventh | **21st** twenty-first | **101st** one hundred (and) first |
| **2nd** second | **12th** twelfth | **22nd** twenty-second | **102nd** one hundred (and) second |
| **3rd** third | **13th** thirteenth | **30th** thirtieth | **1,000th** one thousandth |
| **4th** fourth | **14th** fourteenth | **40th** fortieth | **10,000th** ten thousandth |
| **5th** fifth | **15th** fifteenth | **50th** fiftieth | **100,000th** one hundred thousandth |
| **6th** sixth | **16th** sixteenth | **60th** sixtieth | **1,000,000th** one millionth |
| **7th** seventh | **17th** seventeenth | **70th** seventieth | **1,000,000,000th** one billionth |
| **8th** eighth | **18th** eighteenth | **80th** eightieth | |
| **9th** ninth | **19th** nineteenth | **90th** ninetieth | |
| **10th** tenth | **20th** twentieth | **100th** one hundredth | |

A. What floor do you live on?
B. I live on the _____ floor.

A. Is this your first trip to our country?
B. No. It's my _____ trip.

How many students are there in your class?

How many people are there in your country?

What were the names of your teachers in elementary school? (My *first*-grade teacher was Ms./Mrs./Mr. . . .)

*two o'clock*

*two fifteen / a quarter after two*

*two thirty / half past two*

*two forty-five / a quarter to three*

*two oh five*

*two twenty / twenty after two*

*two forty / twenty to three*

*two fifty-five / five to three*

A. What time is it?
B. It's _____.

A. What time does the movie begin?
B. At _____.

*two A.M.*

*two P.M.*

noon / twelve noon

midnight / twelve midnight

A. When does the train leave?
B. At _____.

A. What time will we arrive?
B. At _____.

Tell about your daily schedule:
  What do you do? When?
  (I get up at _____. I ..............)

Do you usually have enough time to do things, or do you "run out of time"? Tell about it.

Tell about the use of time in different cultures or countries you know:
  Do people arrive on time for work? appointments? parties?
  Do trains and buses operate exactly on schedule?
  Do movies and sports events begin on time?
  Do workplaces use time clocks or timesheets to record employees' work hours?

## Coins

| | Name | Value | Written as: | |
|---|---|---|---|---|
| 1 | penny | one cent | 1¢ | $ .01 |
| 2 | nickel | five cents | 5¢ | $ .05 |
| 3 | dime | ten cents | 10¢ | $ .10 |
| 4 | quarter | twenty-five cents | 25¢ | $ .25 |
| 5 | half dollar | fifty cents | 50¢ | $ .50 |
| 6 | silver dollar | one dollar | | $1.00 |

A. How much is a **penny** worth?
B. A **penny** is worth **one cent**.

A. *Soda* costs *ninety-five cents*. Do you have enough change?
B. Yes. I have a/two/three _____(s) and . . . . . . .

## Currency

| | Name | We sometimes say: | Value | Written as: |
|---|---|---|---|---|
| 7 | (one-) dollar bill | a one | one dollar | $ 1.00 |
| 8 | five-dollar bill | a five | five dollars | $ 5.00 |
| 9 | ten-dollar bill | a ten | ten dollars | $ 10.00 |
| 10 | twenty-dollar bill | a twenty | twenty dollars | $ 20.00 |
| 11 | fifty-dollar bill | a fifty | fifty dollars | $ 50.00 |
| 12 | (one-) hundred dollar bill | a hundred | one hundred dollars | $100.00 |

A. I'm going to the supermarket. Do you have any cash?
B. I have a **twenty-dollar bill**.
A. **Twenty dollars** is enough. Thanks.

A. Can you change a **five-dollar bill/a five**?
B. Yes. I have *five* **one-dollar bills/** *five* **ones.**

| Written as: | We say: |
|---|---|
| $1.30 | a dollar and thirty cents<br>a dollar thirty |
| $2.50 | two dollars and fifty cents<br>two fifty |
| $56.49 | fifty-six dollars and forty-nine cents<br>fifty-six forty-nine |

Tell about some things you usually buy. What do they cost?

Name and describe the coins and currency in your country. What are they worth in U.S. dollars?

1/3/12 JAN 3 2012

 HAPPY 25th

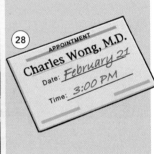
APPOINTMENT
Charles Wong, M.D.
Date: *February 21*
Time: *3:00 PM*

**Days of the Week**    **Months of the Year**

1 year
2 month
3 week
4 day
5 weekend

6 Sunday
7 Monday
8 Tuesday
9 Wednesday
10 Thursday
11 Friday
12 Saturday

13 January
14 February
15 March
16 April
17 May
18 June

19 July
20 August
21 September
22 October
23 November
24 December

25 January 3, 2012
   January third, two
    thousand twelve
26 birthday
27 anniversary
28 appointment

A. What year is it?
B. It's _____.

A. What month is it?
B. It's _____.

[13–24]

[6–12]
A. What day is it?
B. It's _____.

A. What's today's date?
B. It's _____.

[26–28]
A. When is your _____?
B. It's on _____.

Which days of the week do you go to work/school?
(I go to work/school on _____.)

What do you do on the weekend?

What is your date of birth?
(I was born on .....*month day, year*.....)

What's your favorite day of the week? Why?

What's your favorite month of the year? Why?

1 yesterday
2 today
3 tomorrow

4 morning
5 afternoon
6 evening
7 night

8 yesterday morning
9 yesterday afternoon
10 yesterday evening
11 last night

12 this morning
13 this afternoon
14 this evening
15 tonight

16 tomorrow morning
17 tomorrow afternoon
18 tomorrow evening
19 tomorrow night

20 last week
21 this week
22 next week

23 once a week
24 twice a week
25 three times a week
26 every day

**Seasons**
27 spring
28 summer
29 fall / autumn
30 winter

What did you do yesterday morning / afternoon / evening?

What did you do last night?

What are you going to do tomorrow morning / afternoon / evening / night?

What did you do last week?

What are your plans for next week?

How many times a week do you have English class? / go to the supermarket? / exercise?

What's your favorite season? Why?

| 1 apartment building | 5 condominium/condo | 9 shelter | 13 the city |
| 2 house | 6 dormitory/dorm | 10 farm | 14 the suburbs |
| 3 duplex/two-family house | 7 mobile home | 11 ranch | 15 the country |
| 4 townhouse/townhome | 8 nursing home | 12 houseboat | 16 a town/village |

A. Where do you live?

B. I live
- in a/an ___[1–9]___.
- on a ___[10–12]___.
- in ___[13–16]___.

[1–12]

A. Town Taxi Company.

B. Hello. Please send a taxi to
....(address).....

A. Is that a house or an apartment building?

B. It's a/an _____.

A. All right. We'll be there right away.

[1–12]

A. This is the Emergency Operator.

B. Please send an ambulance to
....(address).....

A. Is that a private home?

B. It's a/an _____.

A. What's your name and telephone number?

B. ...........................

Tell about people you know and where they live.

Discuss:
Who lives in dormitories?
Who lives in nursing homes?
Who lives in shelters?
Why?

| | | | |
|---|---|---|---|
| 1 bookcase | 9 VCR / video cassette recorder | 16 speaker | 24 lamp |
| 2 picture / photograph | 10 wall | 17 stereo system | 25 lampshade |
| 3 painting | 11 ceiling | 18 magazine holder | 26 end table |
| 4 mantel | 12 drapes | 19 (throw) pillow | 27 floor |
| 5 fireplace | 13 window | 20 sofa / couch | 28 floor lamp |
| 6 fireplace screen | 14 loveseat | 21 plant | 29 armchair |
| 7 DVD player | 15 wall unit | 22 coffee table | |
| 8 television / TV | | 23 rug | |

A. Where are you?
B. I'm in the living room.
A. What are you doing?
B. I'm dusting* the **bookcase**.

* dusting / cleaning

A. You have a very nice living room!
B. Thank you.
A. Your _____ is / are beautiful!
B. Thank you for saying so.

A. Uh-oh! I just spilled coffee on your _____!
B. That's okay. Don't worry about it.

Tell about your living room.
(In my living room there's ..............)

| | | | |
|---|---|---|---|
| 1 (dining room) table | 10 chandelier | 19 platter | 27 knife |
| 2 (dining room) chair | 11 china cabinet | 20 butter dish | 28 spoon |
| 3 buffet | 12 china | 21 salt shaker | 29 bowl |
| 4 tray | 13 salad bowl | 22 pepper shaker | 30 mug |
| 5 teapot | 14 serving bowl | 23 tablecloth | 31 glass |
| 6 coffee pot | 15 serving dish | 24 napkin | 32 cup |
| 7 sugar bowl | 16 vase | 25 fork | 33 saucer |
| 8 creamer | 17 candle | 26 plate | |
| 9 pitcher | 18 candlestick | | |

A. This **dining room table** is very nice.
B. Thank you. It was a gift from my *grandmother.**

*grandmother/grandfather/aunt/uncle/. . .

**[In a store]**
A. May I help you?
B. Yes, please. Do you have _____s?*
A. Yes. _____s* are right over there.
B. Thank you.

*With 12, use the singular.

**[At home]**
A. Look at this old _____ I just bought!
B. Where did you buy it?
A. At a yard sale. How do you like it?
B. It's VERY unusual!

Tell about your dining room.
(In my dining room there's
.............)

| | | | |
|---|---|---|---|
| 1 bed | 8 electric blanket | 15 curtains | 21 jewelry box |
| 2 headboard | 9 dust ruffle | 16 lamp | 22 dresser/bureau |
| 3 pillow | 10 bedspread | 17 alarm clock | 23 mattress |
| 4 pillowcase | 11 comforter/quilt | 18 clock radio | 24 box spring |
| 5 fitted sheet | 12 carpet | 19 night table/nightstand | 25 bed frame |
| 6 (flat) sheet | 13 chest (of drawers) | 20 mirror | |
| 7 blanket | 14 blinds | | |

A. Ooh! Look at that big bug!
B. Where?
A. It's on the **bed**!
B. I'LL get it.

[In a store]

A. Excuse me. I'm looking for a/an _____.*
B. We have some very nice _____s, and they're all on sale this week!
A. Oh, good!

* With 14 & 15, use: Excuse me. I'm looking for _____.

[In a bedroom]

A. Oh, no! I just lost my contact lens!
B. Where?
A. I think it's on the _____.
B. I'll help you look.

Tell about your bedroom.
(In my bedroom there's ..............)

| | | | |
|---|---|---|---|
| 1 refrigerator | 10 dishwashing liquid | 19 blender | 28 coffeemaker |
| 2 freezer | 11 faucet | 20 toaster oven | 29 trash compactor |
| 3 garbage pail | 12 (kitchen) sink | 21 microwave (oven) | 30 cutting board |
| 4 (electric) mixer | 13 dishwasher | 22 potholder | 31 cookbook |
| 5 cabinet | 14 (garbage) disposal | 23 tea kettle | 32 food processor |
| 6 paper towel holder | 15 dish towel | 24 stove/range | 33 kitchen chair |
| 7 canister | 16 dish rack/dish drainer | 25 burner | 34 kitchen table |
| 8 (kitchen) counter | 17 spice rack | 26 oven | 35 placemat |
| 9 dishwasher detergent | 18 (electric) can opener | 27 toaster | |

A. I think we need a new **refrigerator**.
B. I think you're right.

[In a store]

A. Excuse me. Are your _____s still on sale?

B. Yes, they are. They're twenty percent off.

[In a kitchen]

A. When did you get this/these new _____(s)?

B. I got it/them last week.

Tell about your kitchen.
(In my kitchen there's .............)

| | | | |
|---|---|---|---|
| 1 teddy bear | 9 changing pad | 17 rattle | 25 booster seat |
| 2 baby monitor/intercom | 10 diaper pail | 18 walker | 26 baby seat |
| 3 chest (of drawers) | 11 night light | 19 cradle | 27 high chair |
| 4 crib | 12 toy chest | 20 stroller | 28 portable crib |
| 5 crib bumper/bumper pad | 13 stuffed animal | 21 baby carriage | 29 potty |
| 6 mobile | 14 doll | 22 car seat/safety seat | 30 baby frontpack |
| 7 changing table | 15 swing | 23 baby carrier | 31 baby backpack |
| 8 stretch suit | 16 playpen | 24 food warmer | |

A. Thank you for the **teddy bear**. It's a very nice gift.
B. You're welcome. Tell me, when are you due?
A. In a few more weeks.

A. That's a very nice _____.
Where did you get it?

B. It was a gift from ..............

A. Do you have everything you need
before the baby comes?

B. Almost everything. We're still
looking for a/an _____ and a/an
_____.

Tell about your country:
What things do people buy for a new baby?
Does a new baby sleep in a separate room,
as in the United States?

| 1 | wastebasket | 10 | cup | 19 | hand towel | 28 | shower |
|---|---|---|---|---|---|---|---|
| 2 | vanity | 11 | toothbrush | 20 | washcloth/facecloth | 29 | shower head |
| 3 | soap | 12 | toothbrush holder | 21 | towel rack | 30 | shower curtain |
| 4 | soap dish | 13 | electric toothbrush | 22 | plunger | 31 | bathtub/tub |
| 5 | soap dispenser | 14 | hair dryer | 23 | toilet brush | 32 | rubber mat |
| 6 | (bathroom) sink | 15 | shelf | 24 | toilet paper | 33 | drain |
| 7 | faucet | 16 | hamper | 25 | air freshener | 34 | sponge |
| 8 | medicine cabinet | 17 | fan | 26 | toilet | 35 | bath mat |
| 9 | mirror | 18 | bath towel | 27 | toilet seat | 36 | scale |

A. Where's the **hair dryer**?
B. It's *on* the **vanity**.

A. Where's the **soap**?
B. It's *in* the **soap dish**.

A. Where's the **plunger**?
B. It's *next to* the **toilet brush**.

A. [Knock. Knock.] Did I leave my glasses in there?
B. Yes. They're on/in/next to the _____.

A. *Bobby*? You didn't clean up the bathroom! There's toothpaste on the _____, and there's powder all over the _____!
B. Sorry. I'll clean it up right away.

Tell about your bathroom.
(In my bathroom there's .............)

## Front Yard

1 lamppost
2 mailbox
3 front walk
4 front steps
5 (front) porch
6 storm door
7 front door
8 doorbell

9 (front) light
10 window
11 (window) screen
12 shutter
13 roof
14 garage
15 garage door
16 driveway

## Backyard

17 lawn chair
18 lawnmower
19 tool shed
20 screen door
21 back door
22 door knob
23 deck
24 barbecue/(outdoor) grill

25 patio
26 gutter
27 drainpipe
28 satellite dish
29 TV antenna
30 chimney
31 side door
32 fence

A. When are you going to repair the **lamppost**?
B. I'm going to repair it next Saturday.

[On the telephone]
A. Harry's Home Repairs.
B. Hello.  Do you fix _____s?
A. No, we don't.
B. Oh, okay.  Thank you.

[At work on Monday morning]
A. What did you do this weekend?
B. Nothing much.  I repaired my _____ and my _____.

Do you like to repair things?
What things can you repair yourself?
What things can't you repair?  Who repairs them?

## Looking for an Apartment

1 apartment ads/
  classified ads
2 apartment listings
3 vacancy sign

## Signing a Lease

4 tenant
5 landlord
6 lease
7 security deposit

## Moving In

8 moving truck/
  moving van
9 neighbor
10 building manager
11 doorman
12 key
13 lock

14 first floor
15 second floor
16 third floor
17 fourth floor
18 roof
19 fire escape
20 parking garage

21 balcony
22 courtyard
23 parking lot
24 parking space
25 swimming pool
26 whirlpool
27 trash bin
28 air conditioner

**Lobby**

29 intercom/speaker
30 buzzer
31 mailbox
32 elevator
33 stairway

**Doorway**

34 peephole
35 (door) chain
36 dead-bolt lock
37 smoke detector

**Hallway**

38 fire exit/
   emergency stairway
39 fire alarm
40 sprinkler system
41 superintendent
42 garbage chute/
   trash chute

**Basement**

43 storage room
44 storage locker
45 laundry room
46 security gate

[19–46]
A. Is there a **fire escape**?
B. Yes, there is. Do you want to see the apartment?
A. Yes, I do.

[19–46]

[Renting an apartment]

A. Let me show you around.
B. Okay.
A. This is the _____, and
   here's the _____.
B. I see.

[19–46]

[On the telephone]

A. Mom and Dad? I found an apartment.
B. Good. Tell us about it.
A. It has a/an _____ and a/an _____.
B. That's nice. Does it have a/an _____?
A. Yes, it does.

Do you or someone you know live in an
apartment building? Tell about it.

**A  plumber**
1  The bathtub is leaking.
2  The sink is clogged.
3  The hot water heater
   isn't working.
4  The toilet is broken.

**B  roofer**
5  The roof is leaking.

**C  (house) painter**
6  The paint is peeling.
7  The wall is cracked.

**D  cable TV company**
8  The cable TV isn't working.

**E  appliance repairperson**
9  The stove isn't working.
10  The refrigerator is broken.

**F  exterminator/
   pest control specialist**
11  There are _____ in the kitchen.
   a  termites
   b  fleas
   c  ants
   d  bees
   e  cockroaches
   f  rats
   g  mice

**G locksmith**
12 The lock is broken.

**H electrician**
13 The front light doesn't go on.
14 The doorbell doesn't ring.
15 The power is out in the living room.

**I chimneysweep**
16 The chimney is dirty.

**J home repairperson/ "handyman"**
17 The tiles in the bathroom are loose.

**K carpenter**
18 The steps are broken.
19 The door doesn't open.

**L heating and air conditioning service**
20 The heating system is broken.
21 The air conditioning isn't working.

A. What's the matter?
B. ___[1–21]___.
A. I think we should call a/an ___[A–L]___.

[1–21]
A. I'm having a problem in my apartment/house.
B. What's the problem?
A. _____.

[A–L]
A. Can you recommend a good _____?
B. Yes. You should call ..............

What do you do when there are problems in your home? Do you fix things yourself, or do you call someone?

**A** sweep the floor
**B** vacuum
**C** mop the floor
**D** wash the windows
**E** dust
**F** wax the floor
**G** polish the furniture
**H** clean the bathroom
**I** take out the garbage

**1** broom
**2** dustpan
**3** whisk broom
**4** carpet sweeper
**5** vacuum (cleaner)
**6** vacuum cleaner attachments
**7** vacuum cleaner bag
**8** hand vacuum

**9** (dust) mop/ (dry) mop
**10** (sponge) mop
**11** (wet) mop
**12** paper towels
**13** window cleaner
**14** ammonia
**15** dust cloth
**16** feather duster

**17** floor wax
**18** furniture polish
**19** cleanser
**20** scrub brush
**21** sponge
**22** bucket/pail
**23** trash can/ garbage can
**24** recycling bin

[A–I]
A. What are you doing?
B. I'm **sweep**ing **the floor**.

[1–24]
A. I can't find the **broom**.
B. Look over there!

[1–12, 15, 16, 20–24]
A. Excuse me. Do you sell _____(s)?
B. Yes. They're at the back of the store.
A. Thanks.

[13, 14, 17–19]
A. Excuse me. Do you sell _____?
B. Yes. It's at the back of the store.
A. Thanks.

What household cleaning chores do people do in your home? What things do they use?

| | | | |
|---|---|---|---|
| 1 yardstick | 7 step ladder | 14 fuses | 21 paint |
| 2 fly swatter | 8 mousetrap | 15 oil | 22 paint thinner |
| 3 plunger | 9 masking tape | 16 glue | 23 paintbrush/brush |
| 4 flashlight | 10 electrical tape | 17 work gloves | 24 paint pan |
| 5 extension cord | 11 duct tape | 18 bug spray/insect spray | 25 paint roller |
| 6 tape measure | 12 batteries | 19 roach killer | 26 spray gun |
| | 13 lightbulbs/bulbs | 20 sandpaper | |

A. I can't find the **yardstick**!
B. Look in the utility cabinet.
A. I did.
B. Oh! Wait a minute! I lent the **yardstick** to the neighbors.

[1–8, 23–26]

A. I'm going to the hardware store. Can you think of anything we need?
B. Yes. We need a/an _____.
A. Oh, that's right.

[9–22]

A. I'm going to the hardware store. Can you think of anything we need?
B. Yes. We need _____.
A. Oh, that's right.

What home supplies do you have? How and when do you use each one?

| | | | |
|---|---|---|---|
| 1 hammer | 9 wrench | 16 pliers | 23 router |
| 2 mallet | 10 monkey wrench/ | 17 toolbox | 24 wire |
| 3 ax | pipe wrench | 18 plane | 25 nail |
| 4 saw/handsaw | 11 chisel | 19 electric drill | 26 washer |
| 5 hacksaw | 12 scraper | 20 (drill) bit | 27 nut |
| 6 level | 13 wire stripper | 21 circular saw/ | 28 wood screw |
| 7 screwdriver | 14 hand drill | power saw | 29 machine screw |
| 8 Phillips screwdriver | 15 vise | 22 power sander | 30 bolt |

A.  Can I borrow your **hammer**?
B.  Sure.
A.  Thanks.

* With 25–30, use: Could I borrow some _____ s?

[1–15, 17–24]

A.  Where's the _____ ?
B.  It's on/next to/near/over/under the _____ .

[16, 25–30]

A.  Where are the _____ s?
B.  They're on/next to/near/over/under the _____ .

Do you like to work with tools? What tools do you have in your home?

| A mow the lawn | 1 lawnmower | 8 wheelbarrow | 15 leaf blower |
|---|---|---|---|
| B plant vegetables | 2 gas can | 9 fertilizer | 16 yard waste bag |
| C plant flowers | 3 line trimmer | 10 (garden) hose | 17 (hedge) clippers |
| D water the flowers | 4 shovel | 11 nozzle | 18 hedge trimmer |
| E rake leaves | 5 vegetable seeds | 12 sprinkler | 19 pruning shears |
| F trim the hedge | 6 hoe | 13 watering can | 20 weeder |
| G prune the bushes | 7 trowel | 14 rake | |
| H weed | | | |

[A–H]
A. Hi! Are you busy?
B. Yes. I'm **mow**ing **the lawn**.

[1–20]
A. What are you looking for?
B. The **lawnmower**.

[A–H]
A. What are you going to do tomorrow?
B. I'm going to _____.

[1–20]
A. Can I borrow your _____?
B. Sure.

Do you ever work with any of these tools? Which ones? What do you do with them?

1 bakery
2 bank
3 barber shop
4 book store

5 bus station
6 candy store
7 car dealership
8 card store

9 child-care center/
day-care center
10 cleaners / dry cleaners
11 clinic
12 clothing store

13 coffee shop
14 computer store
15 convenience store
16 copy center

| | | |
|---|---|---|
| 17 delicatessen/deli | 21 drug store/pharmacy | 25 flower shop/florist |
| 18 department store | 22 electronics store | 26 furniture store |
| 19 discount store | 23 eye-care center/optician | 27 gas station/service station |
| 20 donut shop | 24 fast-food restaurant | 28 grocery store |

A. Where are you going?
B. I'm going to the **bakery**.

A. Hi! How are you today?
B. Fine. Where are you going?
A. To the _____. How about you?
B. I'm going to the _____.

A. Oh, no! I can't find my wallet/purse!
B. Did you leave it at the _____?
A. Maybe I did.

Which of these places are in your neighborhood?
(In my neighborhood there's a/an ..............)

1 hair salon
2 hardware store
3 health club
4 hospital

5 hotel
6 ice cream shop
7 jewelry store
8 laundromat

9 library
10 maternity shop
11 motel
12 movie theater

13 music store
14 nail salon
15 park
16 pet shop/pet store

| 17 photo shop | 21 school | 25 toy store |
|---|---|---|
| 18 pizza shop | 22 shoe store | 26 train station |
| 19 post office | 23 (shopping) mall | 27 travel agency |
| 20 restaurant | 24 supermarket | 28 video store |

A. Where's the **hair salon**?
B. It's right over there.

A. Is there a/an _____ nearby?
B. Yes. There's a/an _____ around the corner.
A. Thanks.

A. Excuse me. Where's the _____?
B. It's down the street, next to the _____.
A. Thank you.

Which of these places are in your neighborhood?
(In my neighborhood there's a/an ..............)

| 1 | courthouse | 7 | city hall | 12 | jail | 17 | meter maid |
|---|---|---|---|---|---|---|---|
| 2 | taxi / cab / taxicab | 8 | fire alarm box | 13 | sidewalk | 18 | parking meter |
| 3 | taxi stand | 9 | mailbox | 14 | street | 19 | garbage truck |
| 4 | taxi driver / cab driver | 10 | sewer | 15 | street light | 20 | subway |
| 5 | fire hydrant | 11 | police station | 16 | parking lot | 21 | subway station |
| 6 | trash container | | | | | | |

| | | | |
|---|---|---|---|
| 22 newsstand | 27 pedestrian | 32 bus stop | 37 street sign |
| 23 traffic light / traffic signal | 28 ice cream truck | 33 bus | 38 manhole |
| 24 intersection | 29 curb | 34 bus driver | 39 motorcycle |
| 25 police officer | 30 parking garage | 35 office building | 40 street vendor |
| 26 crosswalk | 31 fire station | 36 public telephone | 41 drive-through window |

A. Where's the _____?
B. On/In/Next to/Between/Across from/ In front of/Behind/Under/Over the _____.

[An Election Speech]

If I am elected mayor, I'll take care of all the problems in our city. We need to do something about our _____s. We also need to do something about our _____s. And look at our _____s! We REALLY need to do something about THEM! We need a new mayor who can solve these problems. If I am elected mayor, we'll be proud of our _____s, _____s, and _____s again! Vote for me!

Go to an intersection in your city or town. What do you see? Make a list. Then tell about it.

**1 child-children**
2 baby / infant
3 toddler
4 boy
5 girl
6 teenager

**7 adult**
8 man–men
9 woman–women
10 senior citizen / elderly person

**age**
11 young
12 middle-aged
13 old / elderly

**height**
14 tall
15 average height
16 short

**weight**
17 heavy
18 average weight
19 thin / slim

20 pregnant

21 physically challenged
22 vision impaired
23 hearing impaired

## Describing Hair

24 long

25 shoulder length

26 short

27 straight

28 wavy

29 curly

30 black

31 brown

32 blond

33 red

34 gray

35 bald

36 beard

37 mustache

A. Tell me about *your brother*.

B. *He's a tall heavy boy* with *short curly brown* hair.

A. Can you describe *the person*?

B. *He's a tall thin middle-aged man.*

A. Anything else?

B. Yes. *He's bald*, and *he* has *a mustache*.

A. What does *your new boss* look like?

B. *She's average height*, and *she* has *long straight black* hair.

A. Can you describe *your grandmother*?

B. *She's a short thin elderly person* with *long wavy gray* hair.

A. Anything else?

B. Yes. *She's hearing impaired.*

Tell about yourself.

Tell about people in your family.

Tell about your favorite actor or actress or other famous person.

| | |
|---|---|
| **1–2** new – old | **25–26** dark – light |
| **3–4** young – old | **27–28** high – low |
| **5–6** tall – short | **29–30** loose – tight |
| **7–8** long – short | **31–32** good – bad |
| **9–10** large/big – small/little | **33–34** hot – cold |
| **11–12** fast – slow | **35–36** neat – messy |
| **13–14** heavy/fat – thin/skinny | **37–38** clean – dirty |
| **15–16** heavy – light | **39–40** soft – hard |
| **17–18** straight – crooked | **41–42** easy – difficult/hard |
| **19–20** straight – curly | **43–44** smooth – rough |
| **21–22** wide – narrow | **45–46** noisy/loud – quiet |
| **23–24** thick – thin | **47–48** married – single |

| | |
|---|---|
| 49–50 rich/wealthy – poor | 61–62 expensive – cheap/inexpensive |
| 51–52 pretty/beautiful – ugly | 63–64 fancy – plain |
| 53–54 handsome – ugly | 65–66 shiny – dull |
| 55–56 wet – dry | 67–68 sharp – dull |
| 57–58 open – closed | 69–70 comfortable – uncomfortable |
| 59–60 full – empty | 71–72 honest – dishonest |

[1–2]
A. Is your car **new**?
B. No. It's **old**.

| | | | |
|---|---|---|---|
| 1–2 | Is your car _____? | 37–38 | Are the windows _____? |
| 3–4 | Is he _____? | 39–40 | Is the mattress _____? |
| 5–6 | Is your sister _____? | 41–42 | Is the homework _____? |
| 7–8 | Is his hair _____? | 43–44 | Is your skin _____? |
| 9–10 | Is their dog _____? | 45–46 | Is your neighbor _____? |
| 11–12 | Is the train _____? | 47–48 | Is your sister _____? |
| 13–14 | Is your friend _____? | 49–50 | Is your uncle _____? |
| 15–16 | Is the box _____? | 51–52 | Is the witch _____? |
| 17–18 | Is the road _____? | 53–54 | Is the pirate _____? |
| 19–20 | Is her hair _____? | 55–56 | Are the clothes _____? |
| 21–22 | Is the tie _____? | 57–58 | Is the door _____? |
| 23–24 | Is the line _____? | 59–60 | Is the pitcher _____? |
| 25–26 | Is the room _____? | 61–62 | Is that restaurant _____? |
| 27–28 | Is the bridge _____? | 63–64 | Is the dress _____? |
| 29–30 | Are the pants _____? | 65–66 | Is your kitchen floor _____? |
| 31–32 | Are your neighbor's children _____? | 67–68 | Is the knife _____? |
| 33–34 | Is the water _____? | 69–70 | Is the chair _____? |
| 35–36 | Is your desk _____? | 71–72 | Is he _____? |

A. Tell me about your ..........
B. He's/She's/It's/They're _____.

A. Do you have a/an _____ ..........?
B. No. I have a/an _____ ..........

Describe yourself.

Describe a person you know.

Describe some things in your home.

Describe some things in your community.

| | | | |
|---|---|---|---|
| 1 tired | 5 hot | 9 full | 13 excited |
| 2 sleepy | 6 cold | 10 happy | 14 disappointed |
| 3 exhausted | 7 hungry | 11 sad/unhappy | 15 upset |
| 4 sick/ill | 8 thirsty | 12 miserable | 16 annoyed |

| | | | |
|---|---|---|---|
| 17 angry/mad | 21 surprised | 25 nervous | 29 proud |
| 18 furious | 22 shocked | 26 worried | 30 embarrassed |
| 19 disgusted | 23 lonely | 27 scared/afraid | 31 jealous |
| 20 frustrated | 24 homesick | 28 bored | 32 confused |

A. You look _____.
B. I am. I'm VERY _____.

A. Are you _____?
B. No. Why do you ask? Do I LOOK _____?
A. Yes. You do.

What makes you happy? sad? mad?

What do you do when you feel nervous? annoyed?

Do you ever feel embarrassed? When?

| 1 apple | 7 apricot | 14 avocado | 20 lemon | 27 dates |
|---|---|---|---|---|
| 2 peach | 8 nectarine | 15 cantaloupe | 21 lime | 28 raisins |
| 3 pear | 9 kiwi | 16 honeydew (melon) | 22 orange | 29 nuts |
| 4 banana | 10 papaya | 17 watermelon | 23 tangerine | 30 raspberries |
| 5 plantain | 11 mango | 18 pineapple | 24 grapes | 31 blueberries |
| 6 plum | 12 fig | 19 grapefruit | 25 cherries | 32 strawberries |
| | 13 coconut | | 26 prunes | |

[1–23]

A. This **apple** is delicious! Where did you get it?

B. At *Sam's Supermarket*.

[24–32]

A. These **grapes** are delicious! Where did you get them?

B. At *Franny's Fruit Stand*.

A. I'm hungry. Do we have any fruit?

B. Yes. We have _____s* and _____s.*

\* With 15–19, use:
  We have _____ and _____.

A. Do we have any more _____s?†

B. No. I'll get some more when I go to the supermarket.

† With 15–19 use:
  Do we have any more _____?

What are your favorite fruits?
Which fruits don't you like?

Which of these fruits grow where you live?

Name and describe other fruits you know.

1 celery
2 corn
3 broccoli
4 cauliflower
5 spinach
6 parsley
7 asparagus
8 eggplant
9 lettuce
10 cabbage

11 bok choy
12 zucchini
13 acorn squash
14 butternut squash
15 garlic
16 pea
17 string bean/green bean
18 lima bean
19 black bean
20 kidney bean

21 brussels sprout
22 cucumber
23 tomato
24 carrot
25 radish
26 mushroom
27 artichoke
28 potato
29 sweet potato
30 yam

31 green pepper/
   sweet pepper
32 red pepper
33 jalapeño (pepper)
34 chili pepper
35 beet
36 onion
37 scallion/green onion
38 turnip

A. What do we need from the supermarket?
B. We need **celery*** and **peas.**†

* 1–15          † 16–38

A. How do you like the
   ___[1–15]___ / ___[16–38]___ s?
B. It's/They're delicious.

A. *Bobby?* Finish your vegetables!
B. But you KNOW I hate
   ___[1–15]___ / ___[16–38]___ s!
A. I know. But it's/they're good for you!

Which vegetables do you like?
Which vegetables don't you like?

Which of these vegetables grow where you live?

Name and describe other vegetables you know.

## Meat

1 steak
2 ground beef
3 stewing beef
4 roast beef
5 ribs
6 leg of lamb
7 lamb chops
8 tripe
9 liver
10 pork
11 pork chops
12 sausages
13 ham
14 bacon

## Poultry

15 chicken
16 chicken breasts
17 chicken legs/
   drumsticks
18 chicken wings
19 chicken thighs
20 turkey
21 duck

## Seafood

**FISH**

22 salmon
23 halibut
24 haddock
25 flounder
26 trout
27 catfish
28 filet of sole

**SHELLFISH**

29 shrimp
30 scallops
31 crabs
32 clams
33 mussels
34 oysters
35 lobster

A. I'm going to the supermarket. What do we need?
B. Please get some **steak**.
A. **Steak**? All right.

A. Excuse me. Where can I find _____?
B. Look in the _____ Section.
A. Thank you.

A. This/These _____ looks/
   look very fresh!
B. Let's get some for dinner.

Do you eat meat, poultry, or seafood?
Which of these foods do you like?

Which of these foods are popular in
your country?

## Dairy Products

1 milk
2 low-fat milk
3 skim milk
4 chocolate milk
5 orange juice*
6 cheese
7 butter
8 margarine
9 sour cream
10 cream cheese
11 cottage cheese
12 yogurt
13 tofu*
14 eggs

\* Orange juice and tofu are not dairy products, but they're usually found in this section.

## Juices

15 apple juice
16 pineapple juice
17 grapefruit juice
18 tomato juice
19 grape juice
20 fruit punch
21 juice paks
22 powdered drink mix

## Beverages

23 soda
24 diet soda
25 bottled water

## Coffee and Tea

26 coffee
27 decaffeinated coffee/decaf
28 instant coffee
29 tea
30 herbal tea
31 cocoa/ hot chocolate mix

A. I'm going to the supermarket to get some **milk**. Do we need anything else?
B. Yes. Please get some **apple juice**.

A. Excuse me. Where can I find _____?
B. Look in the _____ Section.
A. Thanks.

A. Look! _____ is/are on sale this week!
B. Let's get some!

Which of these foods do you like?

Which of these foods are good for you?

Which brands of these foods do you buy?

## Deli

| | | |
|---|---|---|
| 1 roast beef | 7 pastrami | 13 potato salad |
| 2 bologna | 8 Swiss cheese | 14 cole slaw |
| 3 salami | 9 provolone | 15 macaroni salad |
| 4 ham | 10 American cheese | 16 pasta salad |
| 5 turkey | 11 mozzarella | 17 seafood salad |
| 6 corned beef | 12 cheddar cheese | |

## Frozen Foods

18 ice cream
19 frozen vegetables
20 frozen dinners
21 frozen lemonade
22 frozen orange juice

## Snack Foods

23 potato chips
24 tortilla chips
25 pretzels
26 nuts
27 popcorn

A. Should we get some **roast beef**?
B. Good idea. And let's get some **potato salad**.

[1–17]
A. May I help you?
B. Yes, please. I'd like some _____.

[1–27]
A. Excuse me. Where is/are _____?
B. It's/They're in the _____ Section.

What kinds of snack foods are popular in your country?

Are frozen foods common in your country? What kinds of foods are in the Frozen Foods Section?

**Packaged Goods**

1 cereal
2 cookies
3 crackers
4 macaroni
5 noodles
6 spaghetti
7 rice

**Canned Goods**

8 soup
9 tuna (fish)
10 (canned) vegetables
11 (canned) fruit

**Jams and Jellies**

12 jam
13 jelly
14 peanut butter

**Condiments**

15 ketchup
16 mustard
17 relish
18 pickles
19 olives
20 salt
21 pepper
22 spices

23 soy sauce
24 mayonnaise
25 (cooking) oil
26 olive oil
27 salsa
28 vinegar
29 salad dressing

**Baked Goods**

30 bread
31 rolls
32 English muffins
33 pita bread
34 cake

**Baking Products**

35 flour
36 sugar
37 cake mix

A. I got **cereal** and **soup**. What else is on the shopping list?
B. **Ketchup** and **bread**.

A. Excuse me. I'm looking for _____.
B. It's/They're next to the _____.

A. Pardon me. I'm looking for _____.
B. It's/They're between the _____ and the _____.

Which of these foods do you like?

Which brands of these foods do you buy?

**Paper Products**

1 napkins
2 paper cups
3 tissues
4 straws
5 paper plates
6 paper towels
7 toilet paper

**Household Items**

8 sandwich bags
9 trash bags
10 soap
11 liquid soap
12 aluminum foil
13 plastic wrap
14 waxed paper

**Baby Products**

15 baby cereal
16 baby food
17 formula
18 wipes
19 (disposable) diapers

**Pet Food**

20 cat food
21 dog food

A. Excuse me. Where can I find **napkins**?
B. **Napkins**? Look in Aisle 4.

[7, 10–17, 20, 21]

A. We forgot to get _____!
B. I'll get it. Where is it?
A. It's in Aisle _____.

[1–6, 8, 9, 18, 19]

A. We forgot to get _____!
B. I'll get them. Where are they?
A. They're in Aisle _____.

What do you need from the supermarket?
Make a complete shopping list!

| | | | |
|---|---|---|---|
| 1 aisle | 8 shopping cart | 15 express checkout (line) | 22 clerk |
| 2 shopper/customer | 9 (chewing) gum | 16 tabloid (newspaper) | 23 scale |
| 3 shopping basket | 10 candy | 17 magazine | 24 can-return machine |
| 4 checkout line | 11 coupons | 18 scanner | 25 bottle-return machine |
| 5 checkout counter | 12 cashier | 19 plastic bag | |
| 6 conveyor belt | 13 paper bag | 20 produce | |
| 7 cash register | 14 bagger/packer | 21 manager | |

[1–8, 11–19, 21–25]

A. This is a gigantic supermarket!

B. It is! Look at all the **aisle**s!

[9, 10, 20]

A. This is a gigantic supermarket!

B. It is. Look at all the **produce**!

Where do you usually shop for food? Do you go to a supermarket, or do you go to a small grocery store? Describe the place where you shop.

Describe the differences between U.S. supermarkets and food stores in your country.

# CONTAINERS AND QUANTITIES

| | | | |
|---|---|---|---|
| 1 bag | 5 can | 9 head | 14 roll | 18 pint |
| 2 bottle | 6 carton | 10 jar | 15 six-pack | 19 quart |
| 3 box | 7 container | 11 loaf–loaves | 16 stick | 20 half-gallon |
| 4 bunch | 8 dozen* | 12 pack | 17 tube | 21 gallon |
| | | 13 package | | 22 liter |
| | | | | 23 pound |

* "a dozen eggs," NOT "a dozen of eggs"

A. Please get a **bag** of *flour* when you go to the supermarket.
B. A **bag** of *flour*? Okay.

A. Please get two **bottles** of *ketchup* when you go to the supermarket.
B. Two **bottles** of *ketchup*? Okay.

[At home]
A. What did you get at the supermarket?
B. I got _____, _____, and _____.

[In a supermarket]
A. Is this the express checkout line?
B. Yes, it is. Do you have more than eight items?
A. No. I only have _____, _____, and _____.

Open your kitchen cabinets and refrigerator. Make a list of all the things you find.

What do you do with empty bottles, jars, and cans? Do you recycle them, reuse them, or throw them away?

teaspoon
tsp.

tablespoon
Tbsp.

1 (fluid) ounce
1 fl. oz.

cup
c.
8 fl. ozs.

pint
pt.
16 fl. ozs.

quart
qt.
32 fl. ozs.

gallon
gal.
128 fl. ozs.

A. How much water should I put in?
B. The recipe says to add one _____ of water.

A. This fruit punch is delicious! What's in it?
B. Two _____s of apple juice, three _____ of orange juice, and a _____ of grape juice.

an ounce

oz.

a quarter
of a pound
1/4 lb.
4 ozs.

half a pound

1/2 lb.
8 ozs.

three-quarters
of a pound
3/4 lb.
12 ozs.

a pound

lb.
16 ozs.

A. How much roast beef would you like?
B. I'd like _____, please.
A. Anything else?
B. Yes. Please give me _____ of Swiss cheese.

A. This chili tastes very good! What did you put in it?
B. _____ of ground beef, _____ of beans, _____ of tomatoes, and _____ of chili powder.

| | | | | |
|---|---|---|---|---|
| 1 cut (up) | 6 break | 11 combine ___ and ___ | 16 boil | 21 simmer |
| 2 chop (up) | 7 beat | 12 mix ___ and ___ | 17 broil | 22 roast |
| 3 slice | 8 stir | 13 put ___ in ___ | 18 steam | 23 barbecue/grill |
| 4 grate | 9 pour | 14 cook | 19 fry | 24 stir-fry |
| 5 peel | 10 add | 15 bake | 20 saute | 25 microwave |

A. Can I help you?
B. Yes. Please **cut up** the vegetables.

[1–25]
A. What are you doing?
B. I'm _____ing the ..............

[14–25]
A. How long should I _____ the ............?
B. _____ the ............ for ............ minutes/seconds.

What's your favorite recipe? Give instructions and use the units of measure on page 57. For example:

Mix a cup of flour and two tablespoons of sugar.
Add half a pound of butter.
Bake at 350° (degrees) for twenty minutes.

| | | | |
|---|---|---|---|
| 1 ice cream scoop | 10 wok | 19 roasting pan | 28 cookie sheet |
| 2 can opener | 11 ladle | 20 roasting rack | 29 cookie cutter |
| 3 bottle opener | 12 strainer | 21 carving knife | 30 (mixing) bowl |
| 4 (vegetable) peeler | 13 spatula | 22 saucepan | 31 whisk |
| 5 (egg) beater | 14 steamer | 23 colander | 32 measuring cup |
| 6 lid/cover/top | 15 knife | 24 kitchen timer | 33 measuring spoon |
| 7 pot | 16 garlic press | 25 rolling pin | 34 cake pan |
| 8 frying pan/skillet | 17 grater | 26 pie plate | 35 wooden spoon |
| 9 double boiler | 18 casserole dish | 27 paring knife | |

A. Could I possibly borrow your **ice cream scoop**?
B. Sure. I'll be happy to lend you my **ice cream scoop**.
A. Thanks.

A. What are you looking for?
B. I can't find the _____.
A. Look in that drawer/in that cabinet/
   on the counter/next to the _____/
   ..............

[A Commercial]
Come to *Kitchen World*! We have
everything you need for your kitchen, from
_____s and _____s, to _____s
and _____s. Are you looking for a new
_____? Is it time to throw out your old
_____? Come to *Kitchen World* today!
We have everything you need!

What kitchen utensils and
cookware do you have in
your kitchen?

Which things do you use
very often?

Which things do you
rarely use?

| | | | |
|---|---|---|---|
| 1 hamburger | 8 nachos | 15 frozen yogurt | 22 plastic utensils |
| 2 cheeseburger | 9 taco | 16 milkshake | 23 ketchup |
| 3 hot dog | 10 burrito | 17 soda | 24 mustard |
| 4 fish sandwich | 11 slice of pizza | 18 lids | 25 mayonnaise |
| 5 chicken sandwich | 12 bowl of chili | 19 paper cups | 26 relish |
| 6 fried chicken | 13 salad | 20 straws | 27 salad dressing |
| 7 french fries | 14 ice cream | 21 napkins | |

A. May I help you?
B. Yes. I'd like a/an ___[1–5, 9–17]___ /
an order of ___[6–8]___ .

A. Excuse me. We're almost out
of ___[18–27]___ .
B. I'll get some more from the
supply room. Thanks for
telling me.

Do you go to fast-food restaurants? Which ones? How often? What do you order?

Are there fast-food restaurants in your country? Are they popular? What foods do they have?

| | | |
|---|---|---|
| 1 donut | 8 eggs | 15 coffee |
| 2 muffin | 9 pancakes | 16 decaf coffee |
| 3 bagel | 10 waffles | 17 tea |
| 4 bun | 11 toast | 18 iced tea |
| 5 danish/pastry | 12 bacon | 19 lemonade |
| 6 biscuit | 13 sausages | 20 hot chocolate |
| 7 croissant | 14 home fries | 21 milk |

| | |
|---|---|
| 22 tuna fish sandwich | 29 white bread |
| 23 egg salad sandwich | 30 whole wheat bread |
| 24 chicken salad sandwich | 31 pita bread |
| 25 ham and cheese sandwich | 32 pumpernickel |
| 26 corned beef sandwich | 33 rye bread |
| 27 BLT/bacon, lettuce, and tomato sandwich | 34 a roll |
| 28 roast beef sandwich | 35 a submarine roll |

A. May I help you?
B. Yes. I'd like a _____[1–7]_____/ an order of _____[8–14]_____, please.
A. Anything to drink?
B. Yes. I'll have a small/medium-size/ large/extra-large _____[15–21]_____.

A. I'd like a _____[22–28]_____ on _____[29–35]_____, please.
B. What do you want on it?
A. Lettuce/tomato/mayonnaise/mustard/...

Do you like these foods? Which ones? Where do you get them? How often do you have them?

| | | | |
|---|---|---|---|
| **A** seat the customers | **1** hostess | **7** booster seat | **13** salad bar |
| **B** pour the water | **2** host | **8** menu | **14** dining room |
| **C** take the order | **3** diner/patron/customer | **9** bread basket | **15** kitchen |
| **D** serve the meal | **4** booth | **10** busperson | **16** chef |
| | **5** table | **11** waitress/server | |
| | **6** high chair | **12** waiter/server | |

[4–9]
A. Would you like a **booth**?
B. Yes, please.

[10–12]
A. Hello. My name is *Julie*, and I'll be your **waitress** this evening.
B. Hello.

[1, 2, 13–16]
A. This restaurant has a wonderful **salad bar**.
B. I agree.

| | | | |
|---|---|---|---|
| **E** clear the table | **17** dishroom | **23** salad plate | **31** napkin |
| **F** pay the check | **18** dishwasher | **24** bread-and-butter plate | **silverware** |
| **G** leave a tip | **19** tray | **25** dinner plate | **32** salad fork |
| **H** set the table | **20** dessert cart | **26** soup bowl | **33** dinner fork |
| | **21** check | **27** water glass | **34** knife |
| | **22** tip | **28** wine glass | **35** teaspoon |
| | | **29** cup | **36** soup spoon |
| | | **30** saucer | **37** butter knife |

[A–H]
A.  Please _____.
B.  All right.  I'll _____ right away.

[23–37]
A.  Excuse me.  Where does the _____ go?
B.  It goes 
  { to the left of the _____.
  { to the right of the _____.
  { on the _____.
  { between the _____ and the _____.

[1, 2, 10–12, 16, 18]
A.  Do you have any job openings?
B.  Yes.  We're looking for a _____.

[23–37]
A.  Excuse me.  I dropped my _____.
B.  That's okay.  I'll get you another _____ from the kitchen.

Tell about a restaurant you know.  Describe the place and the people.  (Is the restaurant large or small?  How many tables are there?  How many people work there?  Is there a salad bar? . . . )

**APPETIZERS**

1. fruit cup/ fruit cocktail
2. tomato juice
3. shrimp cocktail
4. chicken wings
5. nachos
6. potato skins

**SALADS**

7. tossed salad/ garden salad
8. Greek salad
9. spinach salad
10. antipasto (plate)
11. Caesar salad

**ENTREES**

12. meatloaf
13. roast beef/ prime rib
14. baked chicken
15. broiled fish
16. spaghetti and meatballs
17. veal cutlet

**SIDE DISHES**

18. a baked potato
19. mashed potatoes
20. french fries
21. rice
22. noodles
23. mixed vegetables

**DESSERTS**

24. chocolate cake
25. apple pie
26. ice cream
27. jello
28. pudding
29. ice cream sundae

---

[Ordering dinner]

A. May I take your order?
B. Yes, please. For the appetizer, I'd like the ___[1–6]___ .
A. And what kind of salad would you like?
B. I'll have the ___[7–11]___ .
A. And for the main course?
B. I'd like the ___[12–17]___ , please.
A. What side dish would you like with that?
B. Hmm. I think I'll have ___[18–23]___ .

[Ordering dessert]

A. Would you care for some dessert?
B. Yes. I'll have ___[24–28]___ /an ___[29]___ .

Tell about the food at a restaurant you know. What's on the menu?

What are some typical foods on the menus of restaurants in your country?

1. red
2. pink
3. orange
4. yellow
5. brown
6. beige
7. blue
8. navy blue
9. turquoise

10. green
11. light green
12. dark green
13. purple
14. black
15. white
16. gray
17. silver
18. gold

A. What's your favorite color?
B. **Red**.

A. I like your _____ shirt.
   You look very good in _____.
B. Thank you. _____ is my favorite color.

A. My TV is broken.
B. What's the matter with it?
A. People's faces are _____, the sky is _____, and the grass is _____!

Do you know the flags of different countries?
What are the colors of flags you know?

What color makes you happy? What color makes you sad? Why?

| | | | |
|---|---|---|---|
| **1** blouse | **9** sweater | **15** uniform | **23** tunic |
| **2** skirt | **10** jacket | **16** T-shirt | **24** leggings |
| **3** shirt | **11** sport coat/sport jacket/ | **17** shorts | **25** overalls |
| **4** pants/slacks | jacket | **18** maternity dress | **26** turtleneck |
| **5** sport shirt | **12** suit | **19** jumpsuit | **27** tuxedo |
| **6** jeans | **13** three-piece suit | **20** vest | **28** bow tie |
| **7** knit shirt/jersey | **14** tie/necktie | **21** jumper | **29** (evening) gown |
| **8** dress | | **22** blazer | |

A. I think I'll wear my new **blouse** today.
B. Good idea!

A. I really like your _____.
B. Thank you.
A. Where did you get it/them?
B. At ..............

A. Oh, no!  I just ripped
   my _____!
B. What a shame!

What clothing items in this lesson do you wear?

What color clothing do you like to wear?

What do you wear at work or at school?  at parties?
at weddings?

| | | | |
|---|---|---|---|
| 1 coat | 8 cap | 15 umbrella | 22 ski mask |
| 2 overcoat | 9 leather jacket | 16 poncho | 23 down jacket |
| 3 hat | 10 baseball cap | 17 rain jacket | 24 mittens |
| 4 jacket | 11 windbreaker | 18 rain boots | 25 parka |
| 5 scarf/muffler | 12 raincoat | 19 ski hat | 26 sunglasses |
| 6 sweater jacket | 13 rain hat | 20 ski jacket | 27 ear muffs |
| 7 tights | 14 trench coat | 21 gloves | 28 down vest |

A. What's the weather like today?
B. It's cool/cold/raining/snowing.
A. I think I'll wear my _____.

[1–6, 8–17, 19, 20, 22, 23, 25, 28]
A. May I help you?
B. Yes, please. I'm looking for a/an _____.

[7, 18, 21, 24, 26, 27]
A. May I help you?
B. Yes, please. I'm looking for _____.

What do you wear outside when the weather is cool?/when it's raining?/when it's very cold?

| | | | |
|---|---|---|---|
| 1 pajamas | 7 undershirt/T-shirt | 13 (bikini) panties | 19 stockings |
| 2 nightgown | 8 (jockey) shorts/underpants/ | 14 briefs/underpants | 20 pantyhose |
| 3 nightshirt |    briefs | 15 bra | 21 tights |
| 4 bathrobe/robe | 9 boxer shorts/boxers | 16 camisole | 22 knee-highs |
| 5 slippers | 10 athletic supporter/jockstrap | 17 half slip | 23 knee socks |
| 6 blanket sleeper | 11 long underwear/long johns | 18 (full) slip | |
| | 12 socks | | |

A. I can't find my new _____.
B. Did you look in the bureau/dresser/closet?
A. Yes, I did.
B. Then it's/they're probably in the wash.

What sleepwear items do you wear? What sleepwear items do people in your family wear?

| | | | |
|---|---|---|---|
| 1 tank top | 7 sweatshirt | 13 shoes | 21 sandals |
| 2 running shorts | 8 sweatpants | 14 (high) heels | 22 thongs/ flip-flops |
| 3 sweatband | 9 cover-up | 15 pumps | 23 boots |
| 4 jogging suit/ running suit/ warm-up suit | 10 swimsuit/bathing suit | 16 loafers | 24 work boots |
| 5 T-shirt | 11 swimming trunks/ swimsuit/ bathing suit | 17 sneakers/athletic shoes | 25 hiking boots |
| 6 lycra shorts/ bike shorts | 12 leotard | 18 tennis shoes | 26 cowboy boots |
| | | 19 running shoes | 27 moccasins |
| | | 20 high-tops/high-top sneakers | |

[1–12]
A. Excuse me. I found this/these _____ in the dryer. Is it/Are they yours?
B. Yes. It's/They're mine. Thank you.

[13–27]
A. Are those new _____?
B. Yes, they are.
A. They're very nice.
B. Thanks.

Do you exercise? What do you do? What kind of clothing do you wear when you exercise?

What kind of shoes do you wear when you go to work or to school? when you exercise? when you relax at home? when you go out with friends or family members?

| | | | |
|---|---|---|---|
| 1 ring | 7 chain | 14 suspenders | 21 purse/handbag/ |
| 2 engagement ring | 8 beads | 15 watch/wrist watch | pocketbook |
| 3 wedding ring/wedding band | 9 pin/brooch | 16 handkerchief | 22 shoulder bag |
| 4 earrings | 10 locket | 17 key ring/key chain | 23 tote bag |
| 5 necklace | 11 bracelet | 18 change purse | 24 book bag |
| 6 pearl necklace/pearls/ string of pearls | 12 barrette | 19 wallet | 25 backpack |
| | 13 cuff links | 20 belt | 26 makeup bag |
| | | | 27 briefcase |

A. Oh, no! I think I lost my **ring**!
B. I'll help you look for it.

A. Oh, no! I think I lost my **earrings**!
B. I'll help you look for them.

[In a store]
A. Excuse me. Is this/Are these _____ on sale this week?
B. Yes. It's/They're half price.

[On the street]
A. Help! Police! Stop that man/woman!
B. What happened?!
A. He/She just stole my _____ and my _____!

Do you like to wear jewelry? What jewelry do you have?

In your country, what do men, women, and children use to carry their things?

**Types of Clothing**

1 long-sleeved shirt
2 short-sleeved shirt
3 sleeveless shirt
4 turtleneck (shirt)

5 V-neck sweater
6 cardigan sweater
7 crewneck sweater
8 turtleneck sweater

9 knee-high socks
10 ankle socks
11 crew socks

12 pierced earrings
13 clip-on earrings

**Types of Material**
14 corduroy *pants*
15 leather *boots*
16 nylon *stockings*

17 cotton *T-shirt*
18 denim *jacket*
19 flannel *shirt*
20 polyester *blouse*
21 linen *dress*
22 silk *scarf*
23 wool *sweater*
24 straw *hat*

**Patterns**
25 striped
26 checked
27 plaid
28 polka-dotted
29 patterned/ print
30 flowered/ floral
31 paisley
32 solid *blue*

**Sizes**
33 extra-small
34 small
35 medium
36 large
37 extra-large

[1–24]
A. May I help you?
B. Yes, please. I'm looking for a *shirt*.*
A. What kind?
B. I'm looking for a *long-sleeved shirt*.

* *With 9–16:* I'm looking for _____.

[25–32]
A. How do you like this _____ tie/shirt/skirt?
B. Actually, I prefer that _____ one.

[33–37]
A. What size are you looking for?
B. _____.

Describe your favorite clothing items. For each item, tell about the color, the type of material, the size, and the pattern.

| | | |
|---|---|---|
| 1–2 long – short | 9–10 fancy – plain | 17 stained *collar* |
| 3–4 tight – loose/baggy | 11–12 heavy – light | 18 ripped/torn *pocket* |
| 5–6 large/big – small | 13–14 dark – light | 19 broken *zipper* |
| 7–8 high – low | 15–16 wide – narrow | 20 missing *button* |

21 shorten the *skirt*
22 lengthen the *sleeves*
23 take in the *jacket*
24 let out the *pants*
25 fix/repair the *seam*

[1–2]
A. Are the sleeves too **long**?
B. No. They're too **short**.

| | |
|---|---|
| 1–2 Are the sleeves too _____? | 9–10 Are the buttons too _____? |
| 3–4 Are the pants too _____? | 11–12 Is the coat too _____? |
| 5–6 Are the buttonholes too _____? | 13–14 Is the color too _____? |
| 7–8 Are the heels too _____? | 15–16 Are the lapels too _____? |

[17–20]
A. What's the matter with it?
B. It has a **stained** *collar*.

[21–25]
A. Please **shorten** the *skirt*.
B. **Shorten** the *skirt*? Okay.

Tell about the differences between clothing people wear now and clothing people wore a long time ago.

A sort the laundry
B load the washer
C unload the washer
D load the dryer
E hang clothes on the clothesline
F iron
G fold the laundry
H hang up clothing
I put things away

1 laundry
2 light clothing
3 dark clothing
4 laundry basket
5 laundry bag
6 washer/washing machine
7 laundry detergent
8 fabric softener
9 bleach
10 wet clothing

11 dryer
12 lint trap
13 static cling remover
14 clothesline
15 clothespin
16 iron
17 ironing board
18 wrinkled clothing
19 ironed clothing

20 spray starch
21 clean clothing
22 closet
23 hanger
24 drawer
25 shelf-shelves

[A–I]
A. What are you doing?
B. I'm _____ing.

[4–6, 11, 14–17, 23]
A. Excuse me. Do you sell _____s?
B. Yes. They're at the back of the store.
A. Thank you.

[7–9, 13, 20]
A. Excuse me. Do you sell _____?
B. Yes. It's at the back of the store.
A. Thank you.

Who does the laundry in your home?
What things does this person use?

1 (store) directory
2 Jewelry Counter
3 Perfume Counter
4 escalator
5 elevator
6 Men's Clothing Department
7 customer pickup area

8 Women's Clothing Department
9 Children's Clothing Department
10 Housewares Department
11 Furniture Department/ Home Furnishings Department
12 Household Appliances Department
13 Electronics Department

14 Customer Assistance Counter/ Customer Service Counter
15 men's room
16 ladies' room
17 water fountain
18 snack bar
19 Gift Wrap Counter

A. Excuse me. Where's the **store directory**?
B. It's over there, next to the **Jewelry Counter**.
A. Thanks.
B. You're welcome.

A. Excuse me. Do you sell *ties*?
B. Yes. You can find *ties* in the ___[6, 8–13]___ /at the ___[2, 3]___ on the first/second/third/fourth floor.
A. Thank you.

*ties/bracelets/dresses/toasters/. . .

Describe a department store you know. Tell what is on each floor.

| A | buy | 1 | sale sign | 5 | discount | 9 | regular price |
|---|---|---|---|---|---|---|---|
| B | return | 2 | label | 6 | size | 10 | sale price |
| C | exchange | 3 | price tag | 7 | material | 11 | price |
| D | try on | 4 | receipt | 8 | care instructions | 12 | sales tax |
| E | pay for | | | | | 13 | total price |
| F | get some information about | | | | | | |

A. May I help you?
B. Yes, please. I want to ___[A–F]___ this item.
A. Certainly. I'll be glad to help you.

A. { What's the ___[5–7, 9–13]___?
    { What are the ___[8]___?
B. ___.
A. Are you sure?
B. Yes. Look at the ___[1–4]___!

Which stores in your area have sales? How often?

Tell about something you bought on sale.

1 TV/television
2 plasma TV
3 LCD TV
4 projection TV
5 portable TV
6 remote (control)
7 DVD
8 DVD player
9 video/videocassette/ videotape
10 VCR/videocassette recorder

11 camcorder/ video camera
12 battery pack
13 battery charger
14 radio
15 clock radio
16 shortwave radio
17 tape recorder/ cassette recorder
18 microphone
19 stereo system/ sound system

20 record
21 turntable
22 CD/compact disc
23 CD player
24 tuner
25 (audio)tape/ (audio)cassette
26 tape deck/ cassette deck
27 speakers
28 portable stereo system/boombox

29 portable/personal CD player
30 portable/personal cassette player
31 headphones
32 portable/personal digital audio player
33 video game system
34 video game
35 hand-held video game

A. May I help you?
B. Yes, please. I'm looking for a **TV**.

*With 27 & 31, use: I'm looking for _____.*

A. I like your new _____.
Where did you get it/them?
B. At ....(name of store)....

A. Which company makes the best _____?
B. In my opinion, the best _____ is/are made by .............

What video and audio equipment do you have or want?

In your opinion, which brands of video and audio equipment are the best?

1 telephone/phone
2 cordless phone
3 cell phone/cellular phone
4 battery
5 battery charger
6 answering machine

7 pager
8 PDA/electronic personal organizer
9 fax machine
10 (pocket) calculator
11 adding machine
12 voltage regulator

13 adapter
14 (35 millimeter) camera
15 lens
16 film
17 zoom lens
18 digital camera
19 memory disk

20 tripod
21 flash (attachment)
22 camera case
23 slide projector
24 (movie) screen

A. Can I help you?
B. Yes. I want to buy a **telephone**.*

*With 16, use:* I want to buy _____.

A. Excuse me. Do you sell _____s?*
B. Yes. We have a large selection of _____s.

* With 16, use the singular.

A. Which _____ is the best?
B. This one here. It's made by .....(company).......

What kind of telephone do you use?

Do you have a camera? What kind is it? What do you take pictures of?

Does anyone you know have an answering machine? When you call, what message do you hear?

## Computer Hardware
1 (desktop) computer
2 CPU/central processing unit
3 monitor/screen
4 CD-ROM drive
5 CD-ROM
6 disk drive
7 (floppy) disk
8 keyboard
9 mouse
10 flat panel screen/ LCD screen
11 notebook computer
12 joystick
13 track ball
14 modem
15 surge protector
16 printer
17 scanner
18 cable

## Computer Software
19 word-processing program
20 spreadsheet program
21 educational software program
22 computer game

A. Can you recommend a good **computer**?
B. Yes. This **computer** here is excellent.

A. Is that a new _____?
B. Yes.
A. Where did you get it?
B. At ....*(name of store)*......

A. May I help you?
B. Yes, please. Do you sell _____s?
A. Yes. We carry a complete line of _____s.

Do you use a computer? When?

In your opinion, how have computers changed the world?

| 1 board game | 11 doll house furniture | 21 hula hoop | 31 stickers |
| 2 (jigsaw) puzzle | 12 action figure | 22 jump rope | 32 bicycle |
| 3 construction set | 13 stuffed animal | 23 bubble soap | 33 tricycle |
| 4 (building) blocks | 14 matchbox car | 24 trading cards | 34 wagon |
| 5 rubber ball | 15 toy truck | 25 crayons | 35 skateboard |
| 6 beach ball | 16 racing car set | 26 (color) markers | 36 swing set |
| 7 pail and shovel | 17 train set | 27 coloring book | 37 play house |
| 8 doll | 18 model kit | 28 construction paper | 38 kiddie pool/ |
| 9 doll clothing | 19 science kit | 29 paint set | inflatable pool |
| 10 doll house | 20 walkie-talkie (set) | 30 (modeling) clay | |

A. Excuse me.  I'm looking for (a/an) _____(s) for my *grandson*.*
B. Look in the next aisle.
A. Thank you.

* *grandson/granddaughter/. . .*

A. I don't know what to get my
............-year-old son/daughter
for his/her birthday.
B. What about (a) _____?
A. Good idea!  Thanks.

A. Mom/Dad?  Can we buy
this/these _____?
B. No, *Johnny*.  Not today.

What toys are most popular in your country?

What were your favorite toys when you were
a child?

**A** make a deposit
**B** make a withdrawal
**C** cash a check
**D** get traveler's checks
**E** open an account
**F** apply for a loan
**G** exchange currency

**1** deposit slip
**2** withdrawal slip
**3** check
**4** traveler's check
**5** bankbook/passbook
**6** ATM card
**7** credit card

**8** (bank) vault
**9** safe deposit box
**10** teller
**11** security guard
**12** ATM (machine)/ cash machine
**13** bank officer

[A–G]
A. Where are you going?
B. I'm going to the bank.
   I have to _____ .

[5–7]
A. What are you looking for?
B. My _____ . I can't find it
   anywhere!

[8–13]
A. How many _____ s does the
   State Street Bank have?
B. ............. .

Do you have a bank account? What kind? Where? What do you do at the bank?

Do you ever use traveler's checks? When?

Do you have a credit card? What kind? When do you use it?

## Forms of Payment

1 cash
2 check
   a check number
   b account number
3 credit card
   a credit card number
4 money order
5 traveler's check

## Household Bills

6 rent
7 mortgage payment
8 electric bill
9 telephone bill
10 gas bill
11 oil bill/heating bill
12 water bill
13 cable TV bill
14 car payment
15 credit card bill

## Family Finances

16 balance the checkbook
17 write a check
18 bank online
19 checkbook
20 check register
21 monthly statement

## Using an ATM Machine

22 insert the ATM card
23 enter your PIN number/ personal identification number
24 select a transaction
25 make a deposit
26 withdraw/get cash
27 transfer funds
28 remove your card
29 take your transaction slip/ receipt

A. Can I pay by __[1, 2]__ /with a __[3–5]__ ?
B. Yes. We accept __[1]__ / __[2–5]__ s.

A. What are you doing?
B. { I'm paying the __[6–15]__ .
I'm __[16–18]__ ing.
I'm looking for the __[19–21]__ .

A. What should I do?
B. __[22–29]__ .

What household bills do you receive? How much do you pay for the different bills?

Who takes care of the finances in your household? What does that person do?

Do you use ATM machines? If you do, how do you use them?

1 letter
2 postcard
3 air letter/ aerogramme
4 package/parcel
5 first class
6 priority mail
7 express mail/ overnight mail

8 parcel post
9 certified mail
10 stamp
11 sheet of stamps
12 roll of stamps
13 book of stamps
14 money order
15 change-of-address form

16 selective service registration form
17 passport application form
18 envelope
19 return address
20 mailing address
21 zip code
22 postmark
23 stamp/postage

24 mail slot
25 postal worker/ postal clerk
26 scale
27 stamp machine
28 letter carrier/ mail carrier
29 mail truck
30 mailbox

[1–4]
A. Where are you going?
B. To the post office. I have to mail a/an _____.

[5–9]
A. How do you want to send it?
B. _____, please.

[10–17]
A. Next!
B. I'd like a _____, please.
A. Here you are.

[19–21, 23]
A. Do you want me to mail this letter?
B. Yes, thanks.
A. Oops! You forgot the _____!

How often do you go to the post office? What do you do there?

Tell about the postal system in your country.

1 online catalog
2 card catalog
3 author
4 title
5 library card
6 copier/photocopier/ copy machine
7 shelves
8 children's section
9 children's books

10 periodical section
11 journals
12 magazines
13 newspapers
14 media section
15 books on tape
16 audiotapes
17 CDs
18 videotapes

19 (computer) software
20 DVDs
21 foreign language section
22 foreign language books
23 reference section
24 microfilm
25 microfilm reader

26 dictionary
27 encyclopedia
28 atlas
29 reference desk
30 (reference) librarian
31 checkout desk
32 library clerk

[1, 2, 6–32]
A. Excuse me. Where's/Where are the _____?
B. Over there, at/near/next to the _____.

[8–23, 26–28]
A. Excuse me. Where can I find a/an ___[26–28]___ / ___[9, 11–13, 15–20, 22]___ ?
B. Look in the ___[8, 10, 14, 21, 23]___ over there.

A. I'm having trouble finding a book.
B. Do you know the ___[3–4]___ ?
A. Yes. .............

A. Excuse me. I'd like to check out this ___[26–28]___ /these ___[11–13]___ .
B. I'm sorry. It/They must remain in the library.

Do you go to a library? Where?
What does this library have?

Tell about how you use the library.

| | | | |
|---|---|---|---|
| A police station | I church | 5 firefighter | 13 game room |
| B fire station | J synagogue | 6 emergency room | 14 swimming pool |
| C hospital | K mosque | 7 EMT/paramedic | 15 sanitation worker |
| D town hall/city hall | L temple | 8 ambulance | 16 recycling center |
| E recreation center | | 9 mayor/city manager | 17 child-care worker |
| F dump | 1 emergency operator | 10 meeting room | 18 nursery |
| G child-care center | 2 police officer | 11 gym | 19 playroom |
| H senior center | 3 police car | 12 activities director | 20 eldercare worker/ |
| | 4 fire engine | |     senior care worker |

[A–L]

A. Where are you going?

B. I'm going to the _____.

[1, 2, 5, 7, 12, 15, 17, 20]

A. What do you do?

B. I'm a/an _____.

[3, 4, 8]

A. Do you hear a siren?

B. Yes. There's a/an _____ coming up behind us.

What community institutions are in your city or town? Where are they located?

Which community institutions do you use? When?

| | | |
|---|---|---|
| **1** car accident | **7** kidnapping | **13** blackout/power outage |
| **2** fire | **8** lost child | **14** gas leak |
| **3** explosion | **9** car jacking | **15** water main break |
| **4** robbery | **10** bank robbery | **16** downed power line |
| **5** burglary | **11** assault | **17** chemical spill |
| **6** mugging | **12** murder | **18** train derailment |

**19** vandalism
**20** gang violence
**21** drunk driving
**22** drug dealing

[1–13]
A. I want to report a/an _____.
B. What's your location?
A. ..............

[14–18]
A. Why is this street closed?
B. It's closed because of a _____.

[19–22]
A. I'm very concerned about the amount of _____ in our community.
B. I agree. _____ is a very serious problem.

Is there much crime in your community? Tell about it.

Have you ever experienced a crime or emergency? What happened?

| | | | |
|---|---|---|---|
| **1** head | **9** iris | **17** lip | **25** abdomen | **33** leg |
| **2** hair | **10** pupil | **18** tooth–teeth | **26** breast | **34** thigh |
| **3** forehead | **11** cornea | **19** gums | **27** back | **35** knee |
| **4** face | **12** ear | **20** tongue | **28** arm | **36** calf |
| **5** eye | **13** nose | **21** chin | **29** elbow | **37** shin |
| **6** eyebrow | **14** cheek | **22** neck | **30** waist | |
| **7** eyelid | **15** jaw | **23** shoulder | **31** hip | |
| **8** eyelashes | **16** mouth | **24** chest | **32** buttocks | |

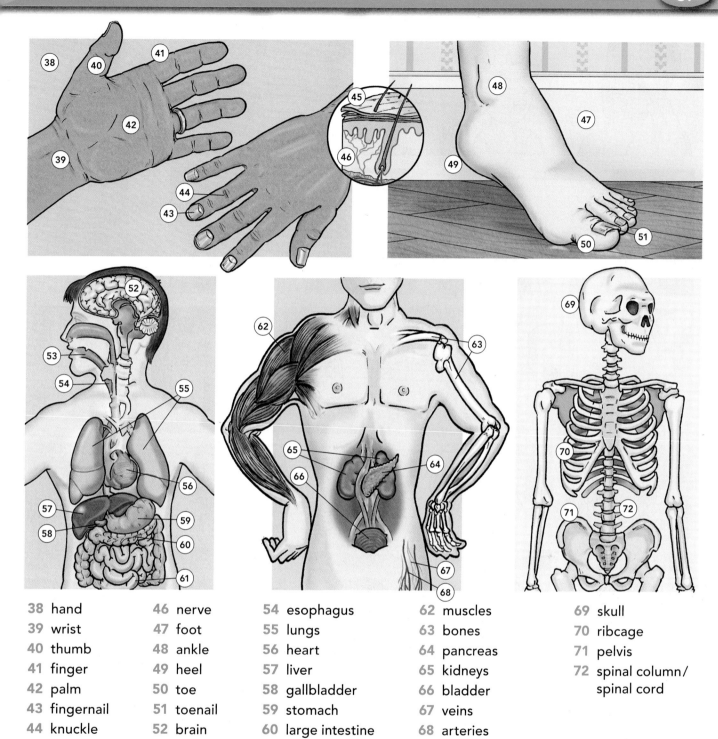

| | | | | |
|---|---|---|---|---|
| 38 hand | 46 nerve | 54 esophagus | 62 muscles | 69 skull |
| 39 wrist | 47 foot | 55 lungs | 63 bones | 70 ribcage |
| 40 thumb | 48 ankle | 56 heart | 64 pancreas | 71 pelvis |
| 41 finger | 49 heel | 57 liver | 65 kidneys | 72 spinal column/ |
| 42 palm | 50 toe | 58 gallbladder | 66 bladder | spinal cord |
| 43 fingernail | 51 toenail | 59 stomach | 67 veins | |
| 44 knuckle | 52 brain | 60 large intestine | 68 arteries | |
| 45 skin | 53 throat | 61 small intestine | | |

A. My doctor checked my **head** and said everything is okay.
B. I'm glad to hear that.

[1, 3–7, 12–29, 31–51]

A. Ooh!
B. What's the matter?
{ My _____ hurts!
{ My _____ s hurt!

[52–72]

A. My doctor wants me to have some tests.
B. Why?
A. She's concerned about my _____.

Describe yourself as completely as you can.

Which parts of the body are most important at school? at work? when you play your favorite sport?

| | | | | |
|---|---|---|---|---|
| 1 headache | 6 sore throat | 11 rash | 17 cavity | 22 cramps |
| 2 earache | 7 fever/ temperature | 12 insect bite | 18 blister | 23 diarrhea |
| 3 toothache | 8 cold | 13 sunburn | 19 wart | 24 chest pain |
| 4 stomachache | 9 cough | 14 stiff neck | 20 (the) hiccups | 25 shortness of breath |
| 5 backache | 10 infection | 15 runny nose | 21 (the) chills | 26 laryngitis |
| | | 16 bloody nose | | |

A. What's the matter?
B. I have a/an ___[1–19]___.

A. What's the matter?
B. I have ___[20–26]___.

| 27 faint | 32 exhausted | 37 vomit / throw up | 42 bruise | 46 sprain |
| 28 dizzy | 33 cough | 38 bleed | 43 burn | 47 dislocate |
| 29 nauseous | 34 sneeze | 39 twist | 44 hurt–hurt | 48 break–broke |
| 30 bloated | 35 wheeze | 40 scratch | 45 cut–cut | 49 swollen |
| 31 congested | 36 burp | 41 scrape | | 50 itchy |

A. What's the problem?
B. { I feel [27–30] .
    I'm [31–32] .
    I've been [33–38] ing a lot.

A. What happened?
B. { I [39–45] ed my ............. .
    I think I [46–48] ed my ............. .
    My ............. is/are [49–50] .

A. How do you feel?
B. Not so good. / Not very well. / Terrible!
A. What's the matter?
B. ............. , ............. , and ............. .
A. I'm sorry to hear that.

Tell about the last time you didn't feel well. What was the matter?

Tell about a time you hurt yourself. What happened? How? What did you do about it?

What do you do when you have a cold? a stomachache? an insect bite? the hiccups?

1 first-aid manual
2 first-aid kit
3 (adhesive) bandage/ Band-Aid™
4 antiseptic cleansing wipe
5 sterile (dressing) pad
6 hydrogen peroxide
7 antibiotic ointment

8 gauze
9 adhesive tape
10 tweezers
11 antihistamine cream
12 elastic bandage/ Ace™ bandage
13 aspirin
14 non-aspirin pain reliever

15 CPR (cardiopulmonary resuscitation)
  a has no pulse
16 rescue breathing
  b isn't breathing
17 the Heimlich maneuver
  c is choking

18 splint
  d broke a finger
19 tourniquet
  e is bleeding

A. Do we have any ___[3–5, 12]___ s/ ___[6–11, 13, 14]___ ?
B. Yes. Look in the first-aid kit.

A. Help! My friend ___[a–e]___ !
B. I can help!
  { I know how to do ___[15–17]___ .
  { I can make a ___[18, 19]___ .

Do you have a first-aid kit? If you do, what's in it? If you don't, where can you buy one?

Tell about a time when you gave or received first aid.

Where can a person learn first aid in your community?

| | | |
|---|---|---|
| 1 hurt/injured | 6 heart attack | 11 get–got an electric shock |
| 2 in shock | 7 allergic reaction | 12 the flu/influenza |
| 3 unconscious | 8 swallow poison | 13 an ear infection |
| 4 heatstroke | 9 overdose on drugs | 14 strep throat |
| 5 frostbite | 10 fall–fell | 15 measles |

| | |
|---|---|
| 16 mumps | 21 diabetes |
| 17 chicken pox | 22 heart disease |
| 18 asthma | 23 high blood pressure/hypertension |
| 19 cancer | 24 TB/tuberculosis |
| 20 depression | 25 AIDS* |

\* Acquired Immune Deficiency Syndrome

A. What happened?

B. My ............ { is ___[1–3]___ .
has ___[4–5]___ .
is having a/an ___[6–7]___ .
___[8–11]___ed. }

A. What's your location?

B. ......(address)...... .

A. My ............. is sick.
B. What's the matter?
A. He/She has ___[12–25]___ .
B. I'm sorry to hear that.

Tell about a medical emergency that happened to you or someone you know.

Which illnesses in this lesson are you familiar with?

**A** measure *your* height and weight

**B** take *your* temperature

**C** check *your* blood pressure

**D** draw some blood

**E** ask *you* some questions about *your* health

**F** examine *your* eyes, ears, nose, and throat

**G** listen to *your* heart

**H** take a chest X-ray

1 scale
2 thermometer
3 blood pressure gauge
4 needle/syringe
5 examination room
6 examination table

7 eye chart
8 stethoscope
9 X-ray machine

[A–H]

A. Now I'm going to **measure your height and weight**.

B. All right.

[A–H]

A. What did the doctor/nurse do during the examination?

B. She/He **measured my height and weight**.

[1–3, 5–9]

A. So, how do you like our new **scale?**

B. It's very nice, doctor.

How often do you have a medical exam?

What does the doctor/nurse do?

**A** clean the wound
**B** close the wound
**C** dress the wound
**D** clean *your* teeth
**E** examine *your* teeth
**F** give *you* a shot of anesthetic/Novocaine™
**G** drill the cavity
**H** fill the tooth

**1** waiting room
**2** receptionist
**3** insurance card
**4** medical history form
**5** examination room
**6** doctor/physician
**7** patient
**8** nurse

**9** cotton balls
**10** alcohol
**11** stitches
**12** gauze
**13** tape

**14** injection/shot
**15** crutches
**16** ice pack
**17** prescription
**18** sling
**19** cast
**20** brace

**21** dental hygienist
**22** mask
**23** gloves
**24** dentist
**25** dental assistant
**26** drill
**27** filling

A. Now I'm going to {
    _____[A–H]_____.
    give you (a/an) _____[14–17]_____.
    put your ............. in a _____[18–20]_____.
}

B. Okay.

A. I need {
    _____[9, 10, 12, 13, 23]_____.
    a _____[22, 26]_____.
}

B. Here you are.

*Tell about a personal experience you had with a medical or dental procedure.*

1 rest in bed
2 drink fluids
3 gargle
4 go on a diet

5 exercise
6 take vitamins
7 see a specialist
8 get acupuncture

9 heating pad
10 humidifier
11 air purifier
12 cane
13 walker
14 wheelchair

15 blood work / blood tests
16 tests
17 physical therapy
18 surgery
19 counseling
20 braces

A. I think { you should _____[1–8]____.
you should use a/an _____[9–14]___.
you need ____[15–20]_____.

B. I see.

A. What did the doctor say?
B. The doctor thinks { I should _____[1–8]____.
I should use a/an _____[9–14]___.
I need ____[15–20]_____.

Tell about medical advice a doctor gave you.
What did the doctor say? Did you follow the advice?

1 aspirin
2 cold tablets
3 vitamins
4 cough syrup
5 non-aspirin pain
  reliever

6 cough drops
7 throat lozenges
8 antacid tablets
9 decongestant spray/
  nasal spray

10 eye drops
11 ointment
12 cream/creme
13 lotion

14 pill
15 tablet
16 capsule
17 caplet
18 teaspoon
19 tablespoon

[1–13]
A. What did the doctor say?
B. { She/He told me to take ____[1–4]____ /a ___[5]___.
    { She/He told me to use ____[6–13]____.

[14–19]
A. What's the dosage?
B. One _____ every four hours.

What medicines in this lesson do you have at home? What other medicines do you have?

What do you take or use for a fever? a headache? a stomachache? a sore throat? a cold? a cough?

Tell about any medicines in your country that are different from the ones in this lesson.

1 cardiologist
2 gynecologist
3 pediatrician
4 gerontologist

5 allergist
6 orthopedist
7 ophthalmologist
8 ear, nose, and throat (ENT) specialist

9 audiologist
10 physical therapist
11 counselor/therapist
12 psychiatrist

13 gastroenterologist
14 chiropractor
15 acupuncturist
16 orthodontist

A. I think you need to see a specialist.
   I'm going to refer you to a/an _____.
B. A/An _____?
A. Yes.

A. When is your next appointment with the _____?
B. It's at ............(time)........... on ............(date)............

Do you or members of your family see any of these medical specialists? Which ones?

**A  patient's room**
1  patient
2  hospital gown
3  hospital bed
4  bed control
5  call button
6  I.V.
7  vital signs monitor
8  bed table
9  bed pan
10  medical chart
11  doctor/physician

**B  nurse's station**
12  nurse
13  dietitian
14  orderly

**C  operating room**
15  surgeon
16  surgical nurse
17  anesthesiologist

**D  waiting room**
18  volunteer

**E  birthing room/
delivery room**
19  obstetrician
20  midwife/nurse-midwife

**F  emergency room/ER**
21  emergency medical
technician/EMT
22  gurney

**G  radiology department**
23  X-ray technician
24  radiologist

**H  laboratory/lab**
25  lab technician

A.  This is your ___[2–10]___.
B.  I see.

A.  Do you work here?
B.  Yes.  I'm a/an ___[11–21, 23–25]___.

A.  Where's the ___[11–21, 23–25]___?
B.  She's/He's { in the ___[A, C–H]___.
                at the ___[B]___.

Tell about an experience you or a family member had in the hospital.

A **brush** *my* **teeth**
1 toothbrush
2 toothpaste

B **floss** *my* **teeth**
3 dental floss

C **gargle**
4 mouthwash

D **whiten** *my* **teeth**
5 teeth whitener

E **bathe / take a bath**
6 soap
7 bubble bath

F **take a shower**
8 shower cap

G **wash** *my* **hair**
9 shampoo
10 conditioner / rinse

H **dry** *my* **hair**
11 hair dryer / blow dryer

I **comb** *my* **hair**
12 comb

J **brush** *my* **hair**
13 (hair) brush

K **style** *my* **hair**
14 hot comb /
   curling iron
15 hairspray
16 hair gel
17 bobby pin
18 barrette
19 hairclip

L **shave**
20 shaving cream
21 razor
22 razor blade
23 electric shaver
24 styptic pencil
25 aftershave (lotion)

M **do my nails**
26 nail file
27 emery board

28 nail clipper
29 nail brush
30 scissors
31 nail polish
32 nail polish remover

N **put on . . .**
33 deodorant
34 hand lotion
35 body lotion
36 powder

37 cologne/perfume
38 sunscreen

O **put on makeup**
39 blush/rouge
40 foundation/base
41 moisturizer
42 face powder
43 eyeliner

44 eye shadow
45 mascara
46 eyebrow pencil
47 lipstick

P **polish my shoes**
48 shoe polish
49 shoelaces

[A–M, N (33–38), O, P]
A. What are you doing?
B. I'm _____ing.

[1, 8, 11–14, 17–19, 21–24, 26–30, 46, 49]
A. Excuse me. Where can I find _____(s)?
B. They're in the next aisle.

[2–7, 9, 10, 15, 16, 20, 25, 31–45, 47, 48]
A. Excuse me. Where can I find _____?
B. It's in the next aisle.

Which of these personal care products do you use?

You're going on a trip. Make a list of the personal care products you need to take with you.

A **feed**
1 baby food
2 bib
3 bottle
4 nipple
5 formula
6 (liquid) vitamins

B **change the baby's diaper**
7 disposable diaper
8 cloth diaper

9 diaper pin
10 (baby) wipes
11 baby powder
12 training pants
13 ointment

C **bathe**
14 baby shampoo
15 cotton swab
16 baby lotion

D **hold**
17 pacifier
18 teething ring

E **nurse**

F **dress**

G **rock**
19 child-care center
20 child-care worker
21 rocking chair

H **read to**
22 cubby

I **play with**
23 toys

A. What are you doing?
B. { I'm ____[A, C–I]____ ing the baby.
    I'm ____[B]____ ing.

A. Do we need anything from the store?
B. Yes. We need some more { ___[2–4, 7–9, 15, 17, 18]___ s
                              ___[1, 5, 6, 10–14, 16]___ .

In your opinion, which are better: cloth diapers or disposable diapers? Why?

Tell about baby products in your country.

1 preschool / nursery school
2 elementary school
3 middle school / junior high school
4 high school

5 adult school
6 vocational school / trade school
7 community college
8 college

9 university
10 graduate school
11 law school
12 medical school

A. Are you a student?
B. Yes. I'm in _____[1–4, 8, 10–12]_____.

A. Are you a student?
B. Yes. I go to a/an _____[5–7, 9]_____.

A. Is this apartment building near a/an _____?
B. Yes. _____(name of school)_____ is nearby.

A. Tell me about your previous education.
B. I went to _____(name of school)_____.
A. Did you like it there?
B. Yes. It was an excellent _____.

What types of schools are there in your community? What are their names, and where are they located?

What types of schools have you gone to?

Where? When? What did you study?

A (main) office
B principal's office
C nurse's office
D guidance office
E classroom
F hallway
  a locker
G science lab

H gym/gymnasium
  a locker room
I track
  a bleachers
J field
K auditorium
L cafeteria
M library

1 clerk/(school) secretary
2 principal
3 (school) nurse
4 (guidance) counselor
5 teacher
6 assistant principal/
  vice-principal
7 security officer

8 science teacher
9 P.E. teacher
10 coach
11 custodian
12 cafeteria worker
13 lunchroom monitor
14 (school) librarian

A. Where are you going?
B. I'm going to the ___[A–D, G–M]___ .
A. Do you have a hall pass?
B. Yes. Here it is.

A. Where's the ___[1–14]___ ?
B. He's/She's in the ___[A–M]___ .

Describe the school where you study English. Tell about the rooms, offices, and people.

Tell about differences between the school in this lesson and schools in your country.

1. math / mathematics
2. English
3. history
4. geography
5. government
6. science
7. biology
8. chemistry
9. physics
10. health
11. computer science
12. Spanish
13. French
14. home economics
15. industrial arts / shop
16. business education
17. physical education / P.E.
18. driver's education / driver's ed
19. art
20. music

A. What do you have next period?
B. **Math**. How about you?
A. **English**.
B. There's the bell. I've got to go.

What is/was your favorite subject? Why?

In your opinion, what's the most interesting subject? the most difficult subject? Why do you think so?

| | | | |
|---|---|---|---|
| 1 band | 5 football | 9 school newspaper | 13 debate club |
| 2 orchestra | 6 cheerleading / pep squad | 10 yearbook | 14 computer club |
| 3 choir / chorus | 7 student government | 11 literary magazine | 15 international club |
| 4 drama | 8 community service | 12 A.V. crew | 16 chess club |

A. Are you going home right after school?

B. { No. I have ___[1–6]___ practice.
{ No. I have a ___[7–16]___ meeting.

What extracurricular activities do / did you participate in?

Which extracurricular activities in this lesson are there in schools in your country? What other activities are there?

## Arithmetic

$$2+1=3 \qquad 8-3=5 \qquad 4\times2=8 \qquad 10\div2=5$$

| addition | subtraction | multiplication | division |
|---|---|---|---|
| 2 **plus** 1 **equals*** 3. | 8 **minus** 3 **equals*** 5. | 4 **times** 2 **equals*** 8. | 10 **divided by** 2 **equals*** 5. |

*You can also say: **is**

A. How much is *two plus one?*
B. *Two plus one* equals/is *three.*

Make conversations for the arithmetic problems above and others.

## Fractions

| one quarter/ one fourth | one third | one half/ half | two thirds | three quarters/ three fourths |
|---|---|---|---|---|

A. Is this on sale?
B. Yes. It's _____ off the regular price.

A. Is the gas tank almost empty?
B. It's about _____ full.

## Percents

| 10% ten percent | 50% fifty percent | 75% seventy-five percent | 100% one-hundred percent |
|---|---|---|---|

A. How did you do on the test?
B. I got _____ percent of the answers right.

A. What's the weather forecast?
B. There's a _____ percent chance of rain.

## Types of Math

$$5y-5y+3=$$

$$\sin(y)=x$$

$$\int_{2}^{6} g(x)\,dx$$

| algebra | geometry | trigonometry | calculus | statistics |
|---|---|---|---|---|

A. What math course are you taking this year?
B. I'm taking _____.

Are you good at math?

What math courses do/did you take in school?

Tell about something you bought on sale. How much off the regular price was it?

Research and discuss: What percentage of people in your country live in cities? live on farms? work in factories? vote in general elections?

## Measurements

1 height
2 width
3 depth
4 length
5 inch
6 foot–feet
7 yard
8 centimeter
9 meter
10 distance
11 mile
12 kilometer

## Lines

13 straight line
14 curved line
15 parallel lines
16 perpendicular lines

## Geometric Shapes

17 square
  a side
18 rectangle
  a length
  b width
  c diagonal
19 right triangle
  a apex
  b right angle
  c base
  d hypotenuse

20 isosceles triangle
  a acute angle
  b obtuse angle
21 circle
  a center
  b radius
  c diameter
  d circumference
22 ellipse/oval

## Solid Figures

23 cube
24 cylinder
25 sphere
26 cone
27 pyramid

---

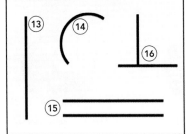

[1–9]
A. What's the ___[1–4]___ ?
B. .................. ___[5–9]___ (s).

[11–12]
A. What's the distance?
B. .................. _____ (s).

1 inch (1″)  =  2.54 centimeters (cm)
1 foot (1′)  =  0.305 meters (m)
1 yard (1 yd.)  =  0.914 meters (m)
1 mile (mi.)  =  1.6 kilometers (km)

[17–22]
A. Who can tell me what shape this is?
B. I can. It's a/an _____.

[23–27]
A. Who knows what figure this is?
B. I do. It's a/an _____.

[13–27]
A. This painting is magnificent!
B. Hmm. I don't think so. It just looks like a lot of _____s and _____s to me!

## Types of Sentences & Parts of Speech

**A** Students study in the new library.
① ② ③ ④ ⑤

**B** Do they study hard?
⑥ ⑦

**C** Read page nine.

**D** This cake is fantastic!

| | | |
|---|---|---|
| **A** declarative | **1** noun | **5** adjective |
| **B** interrogative | **2** verb | **6** pronoun |
| **C** imperative | **3** preposition | **7** adverb |
| **D** exclamatory | **4** article | |

A. What type of sentence is this?
B. It's a/an ___[A–D]___ sentence.

A. What part of speech is this?
B. It's a/an ___[1–7]___.

## Punctuation Marks & the Writing Process

| | | | |
|---|---|---|---|
| **8** period | **12** apostrophe | **16** brainstorm ideas | **19** make corrections/ revise/edit |
| **9** question mark | **13** quotation marks | **17** organize *my* ideas | |
| **10** exclamation point | **14** colon | **18** write a first draft | **20** get feedback |
| **11** comma | **15** semi-colon |   **a** title | **21** write a final copy/ rewrite |
| | |   **b** paragraph | |

A. Did you find any mistakes?
B. Yes. You forgot to put a/an ___[8–15]___ in this sentence.

A. Are you working on your composition?
B. Yes. I'm ___[16–21]___ing.

| 1 fiction | 5 non-fiction | 9 report | 13 letter | 17 thank-you note |
|---|---|---|---|---|
| 2 novel | 6 biography | 10 magazine article | 14 postcard | 18 memo |
| 3 short story | 7 autobiography | 11 newspaper article | 15 note | 19 e-mail |
| 4 poetry/poems | 8 essay | 12 editorial | 16 invitation | 20 instant message |

A.  What are you doing?

B.  I'm writing $\begin{cases} \underline{\hspace{1cm}[1, 4, 5]}. \\ a/an \underline{\hspace{1cm}[2, 3, 6-20]}. \end{cases}$

What kind of literature do you like to read? What are some of your favorite books? Who is your favorite author?

Do you like to read newspapers and magazines? Which ones do you read?

Do you sometimes send or receive letters, postcards, notes, e-mail, or instant messages? Tell about the people you communicate with, and how.

| | | | |
|---|---|---|---|
| 1 forest / woods | 7 plains | 13 dune / sand dune | 19 island |
| 2 hill | 8 meadow | 14 desert | 20 peninsula |
| 3 mountain range | 9 stream / brook | 15 jungle | 21 rainforest |
| 4 mountain peak | 10 pond | 16 seashore / shore | 22 river |
| 5 valley | 11 plateau | 17 bay | 23 waterfall |
| 6 lake | 12 canyon | 18 ocean | |

A. { Isn't this a beautiful _____?!
   { Aren't these beautiful _____s?!
B.   Yes.  It's / They're magnificent!

Tell about the geography of your country.  Describe the different geographic features.

Have you seen some of the geographic features in this lesson?  Which ones?  Where?

## Science Equipment

1 microscope
2 computer
3 slide
4 Petri dish
5 flask
6 funnel
7 beaker
8 test tube
9 forceps
10 crucible tongs
11 Bunsen burner
12 graduated cylinder
13 magnet
14 prism
15 dropper
16 chemicals
17 balance
18 scale

## The Scientific Method

A state the problem
B form a hypothesis
C plan a procedure
D do a procedure
E make/record observations
F draw conclusions

A. What do we need to do this procedure?
B. We need a/an/the _____[1–18].

A. How is your experiment coming along?
B. I'm getting ready to _____[A–F].

Do you have experience with the scientific equipment in this lesson? Tell about it.

What science courses do/did you take in school?

Think of an idea for a science experiment.
What question about science do you want to answer? State the problem.
What do you think will happen in the experiment? Form a hypothesis.
How can you test your hypothesis? Plan a procedure.

## The Universe

1 galaxy
2 star
3 constellation
  a The Big Dipper
  b The Little Dipper

## The Solar System

4 sun
5 moon
6 planet
7 solar eclipse

8 lunar eclipse
9 meteor
10 comet
11 asteroid
12 Mercury
13 Venus
14 Earth
15 Mars
16 Jupiter
17 Saturn
18 Uranus

19 Neptune
20 Pluto
21 new moon
22 crescent moon
23 quarter moon
24 full moon

## Astronomy

25 observatory
26 telescope
27 astronomer

## Space Exploration

28 satellite
29 space station
30 astronaut
31 U.F.O. / Unidentified
   Flying Object /
   flying saucer

[1–24]
A. Is that (a/an/the) _____?
B. I'm not sure. I think it might be
   (a/an/the) _____.

[28–30]
A. Is the _____ ready for
   tomorrow's launch?
B. Yes. "All systems are go!"

Pretend you are an astronaut traveling in space.
What do you see?

Draw and name a constellation you are familiar with.

Do you think space exploration is important? Why?

Have you ever seen a U.F.O.? Do you believe there
is life in outer space? Why?

| 1 accountant | 6 assembler | 10 bricklayer/mason | 15 cashier | 19 construction worker |
| 2 actor | 7 babysitter | 11 businessman | 16 chef/cook | 20 custodian/janitor |
| 3 actress | 8 baker | 12 businesswoman | 17 child day-care worker | 21 customer service representative |
| 4 architect | 9 barber | 13 butcher | 18 computer software engineer | 22 data entry clerk |
| 5 artist | | 14 carpenter | | |

23 delivery person
24 dockworker
25 engineer
26 factory worker

27 farmer
28 firefighter
29 fisher
30 food-service worker

31 foreman
32 gardener/landscaper
33 garment worker
34 hairdresser

35 health-care aide/attendant
36 home health aide/home attendant
37 homemaker
38 housekeeper

A. What do you do?
B. I'm an **accountant**. How about you?
A. I'm a **carpenter**.

[At a job interview]

A. Are you an experienced _____?
B. Yes. I'm a very experienced _____.

A. How long have you been a/an _____?
B. I've been a/an _____ for ............. months/years.

Which of these occupations do you think are the most interesting? the most difficult? Why?

1 journalist/reporter
2 lawyer
3 machine operator
4 mail carrier/letter carrier
5 manager
6 manicurist
7 mechanic
8 medical assistant/physician assistant
9 messenger/courier
10 mover
11 musician
12 painter
13 pharmacist
14 photographer
15 pilot
16 police officer
17 postal worker
18 receptionist
19 repairperson
20 salesperson

21 sanitation worker / trash collector
22 secretary
23 security guard
24 serviceman
25 servicewoman

26 stock clerk
27 store owner / shopkeeper
28 supervisor
29 tailor

30 teacher / instructor
31 telemarketer
32 translator / interpreter
33 travel agent

34 truck driver
35 veterinarian / vet
36 waiter / server
37 waitress / server
38 welder

A. What's your occupation?
B. I'm a **journalist**.
A. A **journalist**?
B. Yes. That's right.

A. Are you still a _____?
B. No. I'm a _____.
A. Oh. That's interesting.

A. What kind of job would you like in the future?
B. I'd like to be a _____.

Do you work? What's your occupation?

What are the occupations of people in your family?

# JOB SKILLS AND ACTIVITIES

1 act
2 assemble *components*
3 assist *patients*
4 bake
5 build *things*/ construct *things*
6 clean
7 cook
8 deliver *pizzas*
9 design *buildings*
10 draw
11 drive *a truck*
12 file
13 fly *an airplane*
14 grow *vegetables*
15 guard *buildings*
16 manage *a restaurant*
17 mow *lawns*
18 operate *equipment*
19 paint
20 play the *piano*

**21** prepare *food*
**22** repair *things*/ fix *things*
**23** sell *cars*
**24** serve *food*

**25** sew
**26** sing
**27** speak *Spanish*
**28** supervise *people*

**29** take care of *elderly people*
**30** take inventory
**31** teach
**32** translate

**33** type
**34** use *a cash register*
**35** wash *dishes*
**36** write

A. Can you **act**?
B. Yes, I can.

A. Do you know how to _____?
B. Yes. I've been _____ing for years.

A. Tell me about your skills.
B. I can _____, and I can _____.

Tell about your job skills.
What can you do?

## Types of Job Ads

1 help wanted sign
2 job notice / job announcement
3 classified ad / want ad

## Job Ad Abbreviations

4 full-time
5 part-time
6 available
7 hour
8 Monday through Friday
9 evenings
10 previous
11 experience
12 required
13 excellent

## Job Search

A respond to an ad
B request information
C request an interview
D prepare a resume
E dress appropriately
F fill out an application (form)
G go to an interview
H talk about your skills and qualifications
I talk about your experience
J ask about the salary
K ask about the benefits
L write a thank-you note
M get hired

A. How did you find your job?
B. I found it through a _____[1–3]_____.

A. How was your job interview?
B. It went very well.
A. Did you _____[D–F, H–M]_____?
B. Yes, I did.

Tell about a job you are familiar with. What are the skills and qualifications required for the job? What are the hours? What is the salary?

Tell about how people you know found their jobs.

Tell about your own experience with a job search or a job interview.

| A | reception area | 1 | coat rack | 11 | swivel chair | 21 | employer/boss | a | take a message |
|---|---|---|---|---|---|---|---|---|---|
| B | conference room | 2 | coat closet | 12 | typewriter | 22 | administrative assistant | b | give a presentation |
| C | mailroom | 3 | receptionist | 13 | adding machine | 23 | office manager | c | sort the mail |
| D | work area | 4 | conference table | 14 | copier/photocopier | 24 | supply cabinet | d | make copies |
| E | office | 5 | presentation board | 15 | paper shredder | 25 | storage cabinet | e | file |
| F | supply room | 6 | postal scale | 16 | paper cutter | 26 | vending machine | f | type a letter |
| G | storage room | 7 | postage meter | 17 | file clerk | 27 | water cooler | | |
| H | employee lounge | 8 | office assistant | 18 | file cabinet | 28 | coffee machine | | |
| | | 9 | mailbox | 19 | secretary | 29 | message board | | |
| | | 10 | cubicle | 20 | computer workstation | | | | |

[A–H]
A. Where's ......(name)......?
B. He's/She's in the _____.

[1–29]
A. What do you think of the new _____?
B. He's/She's/It's very nice.

[a–f]
A. What's ......(name)...... doing?
B. He's/She's _____ing.

Describe a workplace you are familiar with.
Tell about the rooms, the areas, and the employees.

1 desk
2 stapler
3 letter tray /
   stacking tray
4 rotary card file
5 desk pad
6 appointment book
7 clipboard
8 note pad / memo pad
9 electric pencil
   sharpener

10 desk calendar
11 Post-It note pad
12 organizer /
    personal planner
13 rubber band
14 paper clip
15 staple
16 thumbtack
17 pushpin

18 legal pad
19 file folder
20 index card
21 envelope
22 stationery /
    letterhead (paper)
23 mailer
24 mailing label
25 typewriter cartridge
26 ink cartridge

27 rubber stamp
28 ink pad
29 glue stick
30 glue
31 rubber cement
32 correction fluid
33 cellophane tape /
    clear tape
34 packing tape /
    sealing tape

A. My desk is a mess!
   I can't find my ___[2–12]___ !
B. Here it is next to your ___[2–12]___ .

A. Could you get some more
   ___[13–21, 23–29]___ s / ___[22, 30–34]___
   from the supply room?
B. Some more ___[13–21, 23–29]___ s /
   ___[22, 30–34]___ ? Sure. I'd be happy to.

Which supplies and equipment do you use? What do you use them for?

Which supplies in this lesson do you have at home? at school?

| | | | |
|---|---|---|---|
| 1 time clock | 7 line supervisor | 13 forklift | 18 shipping clerk |
| 2 time cards | 8 quality control supervisor | 14 freight elevator | 19 hand truck/dolly |
| 3 locker room | 9 machine | 15 union notice | 20 loading dock |
| 4 (assembly) line | 10 conveyor belt | 16 suggestion box | 21 payroll office |
| 5 (factory) worker | 11 warehouse | 17 shipping department | 22 personnel office |
| 6 work station | 12 packer | | |

A. Excuse me. I'm a new employee.
   Where's/Where are the _____?
B. Next to/Near/In/On the _____.

A. Have you seen *Tony*?
B. Yes. *He's* in/on/at/next to/near
   the _____.

Are there any factories where you live? What kind? What are the working conditions there?

What products do factories in your country produce?

| | | | | |
|---|---|---|---|---|
| **1** sledgehammer | **7** ladder | **13** dump truck | **19** concrete mixer truck | **24** plywood |
| **2** pickax | **8** tape measure | **14** front-end loader | **a** concrete | **25** insulation |
| **3** shovel | **9** toolbelt | **15** crane | **20** pickup truck | **26** wire |
| **4** wheelbarrow | **10** trowel | **16** cherry picker | **21** trailer | **27** brick |
| **5** jackhammer/ pneumatic drill | **11** cement mixer | **17** bulldozer | **22** drywall | **28** shingle |
| **6** blueprints | **a** cement | **18** backhoe | **23** wood/lumber | **29** pipe |
| | **12** scaffolding | | | **30** girder/beam |

A. Could you get me that/those __[1–10]__ ?
B. Sure.

A. Watch out for that __[11–21]__ !
B. Oh! Thanks for the warning!

A. Do we have enough __[22–26]__ / __[27–30]__ s?
B. I think so.

What building materials is your home made of? When was it built?

Describe a construction site near your home or school. Tell about the construction equipment and the materials.

| | | | |
|---|---|---|---|
| 1 hard hat / helmet | 8 safety earmuffs | 14 flammable | 20 biohazard |
| 2 earplugs | 9 hairnet | 15 poisonous | 21 electrical hazard |
| 3 goggles | 10 mask | 16 corrosive | 22 first-aid kit |
| 4 safety vest | 11 latex gloves | 17 radioactive | 23 fire extinguisher |
| 5 safety boots | 12 respirator | 18 dangerous | 24 defibrillator |
| 6 toe guard | 13 safety glasses | 19 hazardous | 25 emergency exit |
| 7 back support | | | |

A. Don't forget to wear your ___[1–13]___!
B. Thanks for reminding me.

A. Be careful!
That material is ___[14–17]___!
That machine is ___[18]___!
That work area is ___[19]___!
That's a ___[20]___! / That's an ___[21]___!
B. Thanks for the warning.

A. Where's the ___[22–25]___?
B. It's over there.

Have you ever used any of the safety equipment in this lesson?
What have you used? When? Where?

Where do you see people using safety equipment in your community?

**A bus**
1 bus stop
2 bus route
3 passenger/rider
4 (bus) fare
5 transfer
6 bus driver
7 bus station
8 ticket counter
9 ticket
10 baggage compartment/
   luggage compartment

**B train**
11 train station
12 ticket window
13 arrival and departure
   board
14 information booth

15 schedule/timetable
16 platform
17 track
18 conductor

**C subway**
19 subway station
20 (subway) token
21 turnstile
22 fare card

23 fare card machine

**D taxi**
24 taxi stand
25 taxi/cab/taxicab
26 meter
27 cab driver/taxi driver

**E ferry**

[A–E]
A. How are you going to get there?
B. { I'm going to take the ___[A–C, E]___ .
    { I'm going to take a ___[D]___ .

[1, 7, 8, 10–19, 21, 23–25]
A. Excuse me. Where's the _____?
B. Over there.

How do you get to different places in your community?   In your country, can you travel far by train or by bus? Where can
Describe public transportation where you live.   you go? How much do tickets cost? Describe the buses and trains.

| | | | |
|---|---|---|---|
| 1 sedan | 7 S.U.V. (sport utility vehicle) | 12 limousine | 17 tractor trailer/semi |
| 2 hatchback | 8 jeep | 13 tow truck | 18 bicycle/bike |
| 3 convertible | 9 van | 14 R.V. (recreational vehicle)/camper | 19 motor scooter |
| 4 sports car | 10 minivan | 15 moving van | 20 moped |
| 5 hybrid | 11 pickup truck | 16 truck | 21 motorcycle |
| 6 station wagon | | | |

A. What kind of vehicle are you looking for?
B. I'm looking for a **sedan**.

A. Do you drive a/an _____?
B. No. I drive a/an _____.

A. I just saw an accident between a/an _____ and a/an _____!
B. Was anybody hurt?
A. No. Fortunately, nobody was hurt.

What are the most common types of vehicles in your country?

What's your favorite type of vehicle? Why? In your opinion, which company makes the best one?

| | | | |
|---|---|---|---|
| 1 bumper | 14 antenna | 26 jack | 38 alternator |
| 2 headlight | 15 rear window | 27 spare tire | 39 dipstick |
| 3 turn signal | 16 rear defroster | 28 lug wrench | 40 battery |
| 4 parking light | 17 trunk | 29 flare | 41 air pump |
| 5 fender | 18 taillight | 30 jumper cables | 42 gas pump |
| 6 tire | 19 brake light | 31 spark plugs | 43 nozzle |
| 7 hubcap | 20 backup light | 32 air filter | 44 gas cap |
| 8 hood | 21 license plate | 33 engine | 45 gas |
| 9 windshield | 22 tailpipe / exhaust pipe | 34 fuel injection system | 46 oil |
| 10 windshield wipers | 23 muffler | 35 radiator | 47 coolant |
| 11 side mirror | 24 transmission | 36 radiator hose | 48 air |
| 12 roof rack | 25 gas tank | 37 fan belt | |
| 13 sunroof | | | |

| | | | |
|---|---|---|---|
| 49 air bag | 58 turn signal | 68 defroster | 77 stickshift |
| 50 visor | 59 steering wheel | 69 power outlet | 78 clutch |
| 51 rearview mirror | 60 horn | 70 glove compartment | 79 door lock |
| 52 dashboard / instrument panel | 61 ignition | 71 emergency brake | 80 door handle |
| 53 temperature gauge | 62 vent | 72 brake (pedal) | 81 shoulder harness |
| 54 gas gauge / fuel gauge | 63 navigation system | 73 accelerator / gas pedal | 82 armrest |
| 55 speedometer | 64 radio | 74 automatic transmission | 83 headrest |
| 56 odometer | 65 CD player | 75 gearshift | 84 seat |
| 57 warning lights | 66 heater | 76 manual transmission | 85 seat belt |
| | 67 air conditioning | | |

[2, 3, 9–16, 24, 35–39, 49–85]

A. What's the matter with your car?
B. The _____(s) is / are broken.

[45–48]

A. Can I help you?
B. { Yes. My car needs __[45–47]__ .
   { Yes. My tires need __[48]__ .

[1, 2, 4–15, 17–23, 25]

A. I was just in a car accident!
B. Oh, no! Were you hurt?
A. No. But my _____(s) was / were damaged.

---

In your opinion, what are the most important features to look for when you buy a car?

Do you own a car? What kind? Tell about any repairs your car has needed.

| | | | |
|---|---|---|---|
| **1** tunnel | **9** underpass | **17** broken line | **25** crosswalk |
| **2** bridge | **10** entrance ramp / on ramp | **18** solid line | **26** intersection |
| **3** tollbooth | **11** interstate (highway) | **19** speed limit sign | **27** traffic light / traffic signal |
| **4** route sign | **12** median | **20** exit (ramp) | **28** corner |
| **5** highway | **13** left lane | **21** exit sign | **29** block |
| **6** road | **14** middle lane / center lane | **22** street | |
| **7** divider / barrier | **15** right lane | **23** one-way street | |
| **8** overpass | **16** shoulder | **24** double yellow line | |

[1–28]

A. Where's the accident?

B. It's on / in / at / near the _____.

Describe a highway you travel on.

Describe an intersection near where you live.

In your area, on which highways and streets do most accidents occur? Why are these places dangerous?

| | | |
|---|---|---|
| 1 over | 5 up | 9 on |
| 2 under | 6 down | 10 off |
| 3 through | 7 across | 11 into |
| 4 around | 8 past | 12 out of |
| | | 13 onto |

[1–8]
A. Go **over** the bridge.
B. **Over** the bridge?
A. Yes.

[9–13]
A. I can't talk right now. I'm getting **on** a train.
B. You're getting **on** a train?
A. Yes. I'll call you later.

What places do you go past on your way to school?     Tell how to get to different places from your home or your school.

## Traffic Signs

1 stop
2 no left turn
3 no right turn
4 no U-turn
5 right turn only
6 do not enter
7 one way
8 dead end/no outlet
9 pedestrian crossing
10 railroad crossing
11 school crossing
12 merging traffic
13 yield
14 detour
15 slippery when wet
16 handicapped parking only

## Compass Directions

17 north
18 south
19 west
20 east

## Road Test Instructions

21 Turn left.
22 Turn right.
23 Go straight.
24 Parallel park.
25 Make a 3-point turn.
26 Use hand signals.

[1–16]
A. Careful! That sign says "**stop**"!
B. Oh. Thanks.

[17–20]
A. Which way should I go?
B. Go **north**.

[21–26]
A. Turn **right**.
B. Turn **right**?
A. Yes.

Which of these traffic signs are in your neighborhood? What other traffic signs do you usually see?

Describe any differences between traffic signs in different countries you know.

**A Check-In**
1 ticket
2 ticket counter
3 ticket agent
4 suitcase
5 arrival and departure monitor

**B Security**
6 security checkpoint
7 metal detector
8 security officer
9 X-ray machine
10 carry-on bag

**C The Gate**
11 check-in counter
12 boarding pass
13 gate
14 boarding area

**D Baggage Claim**
15 baggage claim (area)
16 baggage carousel
17 baggage
18 baggage cart / luggage cart
19 luggage carrier
20 garment bag
21 baggage claim check

**E Customs and Immigration**
22 customs
23 customs officer
24 customs declaration form
25 immigration
26 immigration officer
27 passport
28 visa

[2, 3, 5–9, 11, 13–16, 22, 23, 25, 26]
A. Excuse me. Where's the _____?*
B. Right over there.

*With 22 and 25 use: Excuse me. Where's _____?*

[1, 4, 10, 12, 17–21, 24, 27, 28]
A. Oh, no! I think I've lost my _____!
B. I'll help you look for it.

Describe an airport you are familiar with. Tell about the check-in area, the security area, the gates, and the baggage claim area.

Have you ever gone through Customs and Immigration? Tell about your experience.

1 cockpit
2 pilot / captain
3 co-pilot
4 lavatory / bathroom
5 flight attendant
6 overhead compartment
7 aisle
8 window seat
9 middle seat
10 aisle seat
11 Fasten Seat Belt sign
12 No Smoking sign
13 call button
14 oxygen mask
15 emergency exit
16 tray (table)
17 emergency instruction card
18 air sickness bag
19 life vest / life jacket
20 runway
21 terminal (building)
22 control tower
23 airplane / plane / jet

A take off your shoes
B empty your pockets
C put your bag on the conveyor belt
D put your computer in a tray
E walk through the metal detector
F check in at the gate
G get your boarding pass
H board the plane
I stow your carry-on bag
J find your seat
K fasten your seat belt

[1–23]
A. Where's the _____?
B. In / On / Next to / Behind / In front of / Above / Below the _____.

[A–K]
A. Please _____.
B. All right. Certainly.

Have you ever flown in an airplane?
Tell about a flight you took.

Be an airport security officer! Give passengers instructions as they go through the security area. Now, be a flight attendant! Give passengers instructions before take-off.

| | | | |
|---|---|---|---|
| 1 doorman | 8 front desk | 14 meeting room | 20 hall/hallway |
| 2 valet parking | 9 desk clerk | 15 gift shop | 21 room key |
| 3 parking attendant | 10 guest | 16 pool | 22 housekeeping cart |
| 4 bellhop | 11 concierge desk | 17 exercise room | 23 housekeeper |
| 5 luggage cart | 12 concierge | 18 elevator | 24 guest room |
| 6 bell captain | 13 restaurant | 19 ice machine | 25 room service |
| 7 lobby | | | |

A. Where do you work?
B. I work at the *Grand* Hotel.
A. What do you do there?
B. I'm a/an _____[1, 3, 4, 6, 9, 12, 23]_____ .

A. Excuse me. Where's the ____[1–19, 22, 23]____ ?
B. Right over there.
A. Thanks.

Tell about a hotel you are familiar with. Describe the place and the people.

In your opinion, which hotel employee has the most interesting job? the most difficult job? Why?

**A sew**
1 sewing machine
2 pin
3 pin cushion
4 (spool of) thread
5 (sewing) needle
6 thimble
7 safety pin

**B knit**
8 knitting needle
9 yarn

**C crochet**
10 crochet hook

**D paint**
11 paintbrush
12 easel
13 canvas
14 paint
  a oil paint
  b watercolor

**E draw**
15 sketch book
16 (set of) colored pencils
17 drawing pencil

**F do embroidery**
18 embroidery

**G do needlepoint**
19 needlepoint
20 pattern

**H do woodworking**
21 woodworking kit

**I do origami**
22 origami paper

**J make pottery**
23 clay
24 potter's wheel

**K  collect stamps**
25  stamp album
26  magnifying glass

**L  collect coins**
27  coin catalog
28  coin collection

**M  build models**
29  model kit
30  glue
31  acrylic paint

**N  go bird-watching**
32  binoculars
33  field guide

**O  play cards**
34  (deck of) cards
  a  club
  b  diamond
  c  heart
  d  spade

**P  play board games**
35  chess
36  checkers
37  backgammon
38  Monopoly
  a  dice
39  Scrabble

**Q  go online /
   browse the Web /
   "surf" the net**
40  web browser
41  web address / URL

**R  photography**
42  camera

**S  astronomy**
43  telescope

A.  What do you like to do
    in your free time?
B. { I like to ___[A–Q]___.
   { I enjoy ___[R, S]___.

A.  May I help you?
B.  Yes, please.  I'd like to buy
    (a/an) ___[1–34, 42, 43]___.

A.  What do you want to do?
B.  Let's play ___[35–39]___.
A.  Good idea!

Do you like to do any of these activities in your free time?
Which ones?

What games are popular in your country?
Describe how to play one.

| | | | |
|---|---|---|---|
| 1 museum | 6 historic site | 11 park | 16 planetarium |
| 2 art gallery | 7 national park | 12 beach | 17 zoo |
| 3 concert | 8 craft fair | 13 mountains | 18 movies |
| 4 play | 9 yard sale | 14 aquarium | 19 carnival |
| 5 amusement park | 10 swap meet/flea market | 15 botanical gardens | 20 fair |

A. What do you want to do today?

B. Let's go to { a/an ___[1–9]___.
                 the ___[10–20]___.

A. What did you do over the weekend?

B. I went to { a/an ___[1–9]___.
               the ___[10–20]___.

A. What are you going to do on your day off?

B. I'm going to go to { a/an ___[1–9]___.
                        the ___[10–20]___.

What are some of your favorite places to go? Where are they? What do you do there?

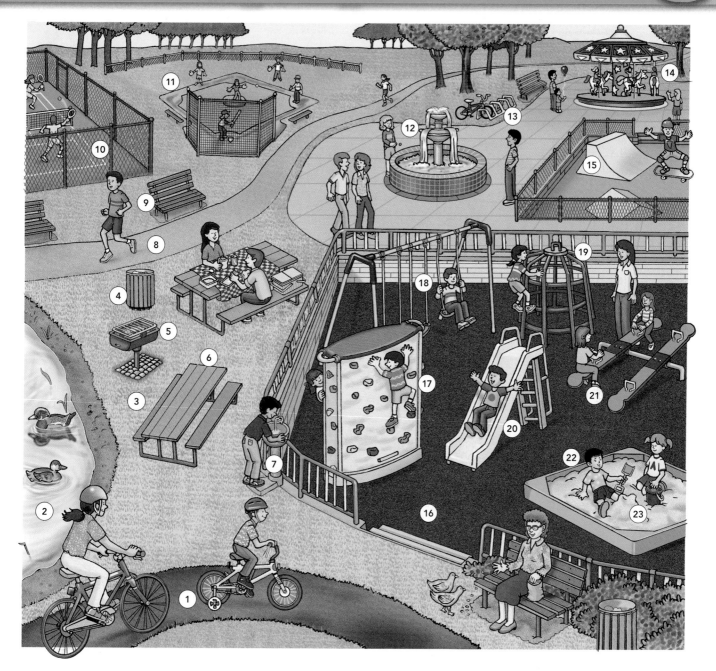

1 bicycle path /
bike path / bikeway
2 duck pond
3 picnic area
4 trash can
5 grill

6 picnic table
7 water fountain
8 jogging path
9 bench
10 tennis court
11 ballfield

12 fountain
13 bike rack
14 merry-go-round /
carousel
15 skateboard
ramp

16 playground
17 climbing wall
18 swings
19 climber
20 slide

21 seesaw
22 sandbox
23 sand

[1–22]
A. Excuse me. Does this park
have (a) _____ ?
B. Yes. Right over there.

[17–23]
A. { Be careful on the ___[17–21]___ !
{ Be careful in the ___[22, 23]___ !
B. I will, Dad / Mom.

Describe a park and playground you are familiar with.

| | | | |
|---|---|---|---|
| **1** lifeguard | **7** wave | **14** sunbather | **21** cooler |
| **2** lifeguard stand | **8** surfer | **15** sunglasses | **22** sun hat |
| **3** life preserver | **9** kite | **16** (beach) towel | **23** sunscreen/sunblock/ |
| **4** snack bar/ | **10** beach chair | **17** beach ball | suntan lotion |
| refreshment stand | **11** beach umbrella | **18** surfboard | **24** (beach) blanket |
| **5** vendor | **12** sand castle | **19** seashell/shell | **25** shovel |
| **6** swimmer | **13** boogie board | **20** rock | **26** pail |

[1–26]
A. What a nice beach!
B. It is. Look at all the _____s!

[9–11, 13, 15–18, 21–26]
A. Are you ready for the beach?
B. Almost. I just have to get my _____.

Do you like to go to the beach? Describe your favorite beach. What do you take when you go there?

**A camping**
1 tent
2 sleeping bag
3 tent stakes
4 lantern
5 hatchet
6 camping stove
7 Swiss army knife

8 insect repellent
9 matches

**B hiking**
10 backpack
11 canteen
12 compass
13 trail map

14 GPS device
15 hiking boots

**C rock climbing /
technical climbing**
16 harness
17 rope

**D mountain biking**
18 mountain bike
19 (bike) helmet

**E picnic**
20 (picnic) blanket
21 thermos
22 picnic basket

A. Let's go ___[A–E]___ * this weekend.
B. Good idea! We haven't gone
   ___[A–E]___ * in a long time.

*With E, say: on a picnic.

A. Did you bring
   { the ___[1–9, 11–14, 16, 17, 20–22]___ ?
   { your ___[10, 15, 18, 19]___ ?
B. Yes, I did.
A. Oh, good.

Have you ever gone camping, hiking, rock climbing, or
mountain biking? Tell about it: What did you do? Where?
What equipment did you use?

Do you like to go on picnics? Where?
What picnic supplies and food do you take with you?

**A  jogging**
1  jogging suit
2  jogging shoes

**B  running**
3  running shorts
4  running shoes

**C  walking**
5  walking shoes

**D  inline skating / rollerblading**
6  inline skates / rollerblades
7  knee pads

**E  cycling / biking**
8  bicycle / bike
9  (bicycle / bike) helmet

**F  skateboarding**
10  skateboard
11  elbow pads

**G  bowling**
12  bowling ball
13  bowling shoes

**H  horseback riding**
14  saddle
15  reins
16  stirrups

**I  tennis**
17  tennis racket
18  tennis ball
19  tennis shorts

**J  badminton**
20  badminton racket
21  birdie / shuttlecock

**K  racquetball**
22  safety goggles
23  racquetball
24  racquet

**L  table tennis / ping pong**
25  paddle
26  ping pong table
27  net
28  ping pong ball

**M golf**
29 golf clubs
30 golf ball

**N Frisbee**
31 Frisbee/flying disc

**O billiards/pool**
32 pool table
33 pool stick
34 billiard balls

**P martial arts**
35 black belt

**Q gymnastics**
36 horse
37 parallel bars
38 mat
39 balance beam
40 trampoline

**R weightlifting**
41 barbell
42 weights

**S archery**
43 bow and arrow
44 target

**T box**
45 boxing gloves
46 (boxing) trunks

**U wrestle**
47 wrestling uniform
48 (wrestling) mat

**V work out/exercise**
49 treadmill
50 rowing machine
51 exercise bike
52 universal/
   exercise equipment

[A–V]
A. What do you like to do in your free time?
B. {
   I like to go __[A–H]__ .
   I like to play __[I–O]__ .
   I like to do __[P–S]__ .
   I like to __[T–V]__ .
}

[1–52]
A. I really like this/these new _____ .
B. It's/They're very nice.

Do you do any of these activities? Which ones?
Which are popular in your country?

**A  baseball**
1  baseball player
2  baseball field / ballfield

**B  softball**
3  softball player
4  ballfield

**C  football**
5  football player
6  football field

**D  lacrosse**
7  lacrosse player
8  lacrosse field

**E  (ice) hockey**
9  hockey player
10  hockey rink

**F  basketball**
11  basketball player
12  basketball court

**G  volleyball**
13  volleyball player
14  volleyball court

**H  soccer**
15  soccer player
16  soccer field

[A–H]
A.  Do you like to play **baseball**?
B.  Yes.  **Baseball** is one of my favorite sports.

A.  ............. plays  [A–H]  very well.
B.  You're right.  I think he's/she's one
   of the best _____s* on the team.

*Use 1, 3, 5, 7, 9, 11, 13, 15.

A.  Now listen, team!  I want all of you
   to go out on that _____† and play
   the best game of  [A–H]  you've
   ever played!
B.  All right, Coach!

† Use 2, 4, 6, 8, 10, 12, 14, 16.

Which sports in this lesson do you like
to play?  Which do you like to watch?

What are your favorite teams?

Name some famous players of these
sports.

**A baseball**
1 baseball
2 bat
3 batting helmet
4 (baseball) uniform
5 catcher's mask
6 (baseball) glove
7 catcher's mitt

**B softball**
8 softball
9 softball glove

**C football**
10 football
11 football helmet
12 shoulder pads

**D lacrosse**
13 lacrosse ball
14 face guard
15 lacrosse stick

**E (ice) hockey**
16 hockey puck
17 hockey stick
18 hockey mask
19 hockey glove
20 hockey skates

**F basketball**
21 basketball
22 backboard
23 basketball hoop

**G volleyball**
24 volleyball
25 volleyball net

**H soccer**
26 soccer ball
27 shinguards

[1–27]
A. I can't find my **baseball**!
B. Look in the closet.*

*closet, basement, garage

[In a store]
A. Excuse me. I'm looking for (a) __[1–27]__.
B. All our __[A–H]__ equipment is over there.
A. Thanks.

[At home]
A. I'm going to play __[A–H]__ after school today.
B. Don't forget your __[1–21, 24, 26, 27]__ !

Which sports in this lesson are popular in your country? Which sports do students play in high school?

**A (downhill) skiing**
1 skis
2 ski boots
3 bindings
4 (ski) poles

**B cross-country skiing**
5 cross-country skis

**C (ice) skating**
6 (ice) skates
7 blade
8 skate guard

**D figure skating**
9 figure skates

**E snowboarding**
10 snowboard

**F sledding**
11 sled
12 sledding dish / saucer

**G bobsledding**
13 bobsled

**H snowmobiling**
14 snowmobile

[A–H]
A. What's your favorite winter sport?
B. **Skiing**.

[A–H]
  [At work or at school on Friday]
A. What are you going to do this weekend?
B. I'm going to go _____.

[1–14]
  [On the telephone]
A. Hello. *Sally's* Sporting Goods.
B. Hello. Do you sell _____(s)?
A. Yes, we do. / No, we don't.

Have you ever done any of these activities? Which ones?

Have you ever watched the Winter Olympics? Which event do you think is the most exciting? the most dangerous?

| A | **sailing** | D | **kayaking** | F | **swimming** | H | **scuba diving** | K | **waterskiing** |
|---|---|---|---|---|---|---|---|---|---|

**A sailing**
1 sailboat
2 life jacket / life vest

**B canoeing**
3 canoe
4 paddles

**C rowing**
5 rowboat
6 oars

**D kayaking**
7 kayak
8 paddles

**E (white-water) rafting**
9 raft
10 life jacket / life vest

**F swimming**
11 swimsuit / bathing suit
12 goggles
13 bathing cap

**G snorkeling**
14 mask
15 snorkel
16 fins

**H scuba diving**
17 wet suit
18 (air) tank
19 (diving) mask

**I surfing**
20 surfboard

**J windsurfing**
21 sailboard
22 sail

**K waterskiing**
23 water skis
24 towrope

**L fishing**
25 (fishing) rod / pole
26 reel
27 (fishing) line
28 (fishing) net
29 bait

[A–L]
A. Would you like to go **sailing** tomorrow?
B. Sure. I'd love to.

A. Have you ever gone __[A–L]__ ?
B. Yes, I have. / No, I haven't.

A. Do you have everything you need to go __[A–L]__ ?
B. Yes. I have my __[1–29]__ (and my __[1–29]__ ).
A. Have a good time!

Which sports in this lesson have you tried?
Which sports would you like to try?

Are any of these sports popular in your country? Which ones?

| | | | |
|---|---|---|---|
| 1 hit | 7 serve | 13 walk | 19 swing | 25 sit-up |
| 2 pitch | 8 bounce | 14 run | 20 lift | 26 deep knee bend |
| 3 throw | 9 dribble | 15 hop | 21 swim | 27 jumping jack |
| 4 catch | 10 shoot | 16 skip | 22 dive | 28 somersault |
| 5 pass | 11 stretch | 17 jump | 23 shoot | 29 cartwheel |
| 6 kick | 12 bend | 18 reach | 24 push-up | 30 handstand |

[1–10]
A. _____ the ball!
B. Okay, Coach!

[11–23]
A. Now _____!
B. Like this?
A. Yes.

[24–30]
A. Okay, everybody. I want you to do twenty _____s!
B. Twenty _____s?!
A. That's right.

Do you exercise regularly?
Which exercises do you do?

Be an exercise instructor! Lead your friends in an exercise routine using the actions in this lesson.

**A  play**
1  theater
2  actor
3  actress

**B  concert**
4  concert hall
5  orchestra
6  musician
7  conductor
8  band

**C  opera**
9  opera singer

**D  ballet**
10  ballet dancer
11  ballerina

**E  music club**
12  singer

**F  movies**
13  (movie) theater
14  (movie) screen
15  actress
16  actor

**G  comedy club**
17  comedian

[A–G]
A.  What are you doing this evening?
B.  I'm going to { a _____[A, B, E, G]_____.
                   the _____[C, D, F]_____.

[1–17]
A.  What a magnificent _____!
B.  I agree.

What kinds of entertainment in this lesson do you like?
What kinds of entertainment are popular in your country?

Who are some of your favorite actors?  actresses?
musicians?  singers?  comedians?

**A**

| A music | | | B plays |
|---|---|---|---|
| 1 classical music | 5 folk music | 9 blues | 13 drama |
| 2 popular music | 6 rap music | 10 bluegrass | 14 comedy |
| 3 country music | 7 gospel music | 11 hip hop | 15 tragedy |
| 4 rock music | 8 jazz | 12 reggae | 16 musical (comedy) |

## C movies/films

17 drama
18 comedy
19 western
20 mystery
21 musical
22 cartoon
23 documentary

24 action movie/ adventure movie
25 war movie
26 horror movie
27 science fiction movie
28 foreign film

## D TV programs

29 drama
30 (situation) comedy/ sitcom
31 talk show
32 game show/quiz show
33 reality show
34 soap opera

35 cartoon
36 children's program
37 news program
38 sports program
39 nature program
40 shopping program

A. What kind of ___[A–D]___ do you like?
B. { I like ___[1–12]___.
   { I like ___[13–40]___s.

What's your favorite type of music?
Who is your favorite singer? musician? musical group?

What kind of movies do you like?
Who are your favorite movie stars?
What are the titles of your favorite movies?

What kind of TV programs do you like?
What are your favorite shows?

**Strings**
1 violin
2 viola
3 cello
4 bass
5 (acoustic) guitar
6 electric guitar
7 banjo
8 harp

**Woodwinds**
9 piccolo
10 flute
11 clarinet
12 oboe
13 recorder
14 saxophone
15 bassoon

**Brass**
16 trumpet
17 trombone
18 French horn
19 tuba

**Percussion**
20 drums
  a cymbals
21 tambourine
22 xylophone

**Keyboard Instruments**
23 piano
24 electric keyboard
25 organ

**Other Instruments**
26 accordion
27 harmonica

A. Do you play a musical instrument?
B. Yes. I play the **violin**.

A. You play the **trumpet** very well.
B. Thank you.

A. What's that noise?!
B. That's my son/daughter practicing the **drums**.

Do you play a musical instrument? Which one?

Which instruments are usually in an orchestra? a marching band? a rock group?

Name and describe typical musical instruments in your country.

| | | | | |
|---|---|---|---|---|
| 1 farmhouse | 9 horse | 16 pig | 23 tractor | 30 farm worker |
| 2 farmer | 10 barnyard | 17 chicken coop | 24 field | 31 alfalfa |
| 3 (vegetable) garden | 11 turkey | 18 chicken | 25 pasture | 32 corn |
| 4 scarecrow | 12 goat | 19 hen house | 26 cow | 33 cotton |
| 5 hay | 13 lamb | 20 hen | 27 sheep | 34 rice |
| 6 hired hand | 14 rooster | 21 crop | 28 orchard | 35 soybeans |
| 7 barn | 15 pig pen | 22 irrigation system | 29 fruit tree | 36 wheat |
| 8 stable | | | | |

[1–30]

A. Where's the _____?
B. In / Next to the _____.

A. The __[9, 11–14, 16, 18, 20, 26]__ s / __[27]__ are loose again!
B. Oh, no! Where are they?
A. They're in the __[1, 3, 7, 8, 10, 15, 17, 19, 24, 25, 28]__.

[31–36]

A. Do you grow _____ on your farm?
B. No. We grow _____.

Tell about farms in your country. What crops and animals are common on these farms?

1 moose
   a antler
2 polar bear
3 deer
   a hoof-hooves
4 wolf-wolves
   a coat/fur
5 (black) bear
   a claw
6 mountain lion
7 (grizzly) bear

8 buffalo/bison
9 coyote
10 fox
11 skunk
12 porcupine
   a quill
13 rabbit
14 beaver
15 raccoon
16 possum/opossum

17 horse
   a tail
18 pony
19 donkey
20 armadillo
21 bat
22 worm
23 slug
24 monkey
25 anteater
26 llama

27 jaguar
   a spots
28 mouse-mice
29 rat
30 chipmunk
31 squirrel
32 gopher
33 prairie dog
34 cat
   a whiskers

35 kitten
36 dog
37 puppy
38 hamster
39 gerbil
40 guinea pig
41 goldfish
42 canary
43 parakeet

| 44 antelope | 49 panther | 53 elephant | 56 giraffe | 61 gorilla |
| 45 baboon | 50 gibbon |   a tusk | 57 zebra | 62 kangaroo |
| 46 rhinoceros | 51 tiger |   b trunk |   a stripes |   a pouch |
|   a horn |   a paw | 54 hyena | 58 chimpanzee | 63 koala (bear) |
| 47 panda | 52 camel | 55 lion | 59 hippopotamus | 64 platypus |
| 48 orangutan |   a hump |   a mane | 60 leopard | |

[1–33, 44–64]
A. Look at that _____!
B. Wow! That's the biggest _____ I've ever seen!

[34–43]
A. Do you have a pet?
B. Yes. I have a _____.
A. What's your _____'s name?
B. ...............

What animals are there where you live?

Is there a zoo near where you live? What animals does it have?

What are some common pets in your country?

If you could be an animal, which animal would you like to be? Why?

Does your culture have any popular folk tales or children's stories about animals? Tell a story you know.

## Birds

1 robin
  a nest
  b egg
2 blue jay
  a wing
  b tail
  c feather
3 cardinal
4 crow
5 seagull

6 woodpecker
  a beak
7 pigeon
8 owl
9 hawk
10 eagle
  a claw
11 swan
12 hummingbird
13 duck
  a bill

14 sparrow
15 goose-geese
16 penguin
17 flamingo
18 crane
19 stork
20 pelican
21 peacock
22 parrot
23 ostrich

## Insects

24 fly
25 ladybug
26 firefly/
  lightning bug
27 moth
28 caterpillar
  a cocoon
29 butterfly
30 tick
31 mosquito
32 dragonfly

33 spider
  a web
34 praying mantis
35 wasp
36 bee
  a beehive
37 grasshopper
38 beetle
39 scorpion
40 centipede
41 cricket

[1–41]
A. Is that a/an _____?
B. No. I think it's a/an
  _____.

[24–41]
A. Hold still! There's a _____ on your shirt!
B. Oh! Can you get it off me?
A. There! It's gone!

What birds and insects are there where you live?

Does your culture have any popular folk tales or children's stories about birds or insects? Tell a story you know.

### Fish

1 trout
  a fin
  b gill
  c scales
2 flounder
3 tuna
4 swordfish
5 bass
6 shark
7 eel

8 cod
9 ray/stingray
10 sea horse

### Sea Animals

11 whale
12 dolphin
13 porpoise
14 jellyfish
15 octopus
  a tentacle

16 seal
17 sea lion
18 otter
19 walrus
  a tusk
20 crab
21 squid
22 snail
23 starfish
24 sea urchin
25 sea anemone

### Amphibians and Reptiles

26 tortoise
  a shell
27 turtle
28 alligator
29 crocodile
30 lizard
31 iguana
32 frog

33 newt
34 salamander
35 toad
36 snake
37 rattlesnake
38 boa constrictor
39 cobra

[1–39]
A. Is that a/an _____?
B. No. I think it's a/an _____.

[26–39]
A. Are there any _____s around here?
B. No. But there are lots of _____!

What fish, sea animals, and reptiles can be found in your country? Which ones are endangered and need to be protected? Why?

In your opinion, which ones are the most interesting? the most beautiful? the most dangerous?

| | | | |
|---|---|---|---|
| **1** tree | **8** root | **14** elm | **21** redwood | **28** plant |
| **2** leaf-leaves | **9** needle | **15** cherry | **22** (weeping) willow | **29** cactus-cacti |
| **3** twig | **10** pine cone | **16** palm | **23** bush | **30** vine |
| **4** branch | | **17** birch | **24** holly | **31** poison ivy |
| **5** limb | **11** dogwood | **18** maple | **25** berries | **32** poison sumac |
| **6** trunk | **12** holly | **19** oak | **26** shrub | **33** poison oak |
| **7** bark | **13** magnolia | **20** pine | **27** fern | |

| | | | | |
|---|---|---|---|---|
| 34 flower | 40 chrysanthemum | 45 gardenia | 50 orchid | 55 geranium |
| 35 petal | 41 daffodil | 46 lily | 51 rose | 56 violet |
| 36 stem | 42 daisy | 47 iris | 52 sunflower | 57 poinsettia |
| 37 bud | 43 marigold | 48 pansy | 53 crocus | 58 jasmine |
| 38 thorn | 44 carnation | 49 petunia | 54 tulip | 59 hibiscus |
| 39 bulb | | | | |

[11–22]
A.  What kind of tree is that?
B.  I think it's a/an _____ tree.

[31–33]
A.  Watch out for the _____ over there!
B.  Oh.  Thanks for the warning.

[40–57]
A.  Look at all the _____s!*
B.  They're beautiful!

*With 58 and 59, use: Look at all the ___!

Describe your favorite tree and your favorite flower.

What kinds of trees and flowers grow where you live?

In your country, what flowers do you see at weddings? at funerals? during holidays? in hospital rooms? Tell which flowers people use for different occasions.

TURN LIGHTS
OFF WHEN
NOT IN USE

## Sources of Energy

1 oil/petroleum
2 (natural) gas
3 coal
4 nuclear energy
5 solar energy
6 hydroelectric power
7 wind
8 geothermal energy

## Conservation

9 recycle
10 save energy/ conserve energy
11 save water/ conserve water
12 carpool

## Environmental Problems

13 air pollution
14 water pollution
15 hazardous waste/ toxic waste
16 acid rain
17 radiation
18 global warming

[1–8]
A. In my opinion, _____ will be our best source of energy in the future.
B. I disagree. I think our best source of energy will be _____.

[9–12]
A. Do you _____?
B. Yes. I'm very concerned about the environment.

[13–18]
A. Do you worry about the environment?
B. Yes. I'm very concerned about _____.

What kind of energy do you use to heat your home? to cook? In your opinion, which will be the best source of energy in the future?

Do you practice conservation? What do you do to help the environment?

In your opinion, what is the most serious environmental problem in the world today? Why?

| | | | | |
|---|---|---|---|---|
| **1** earthquake | **4** blizzard | **7** tsunami | **9** forest fire | **12** mudslide |
| **2** hurricane | **5** tornado | **8** drought | **10** wildfire | **13** avalanche |
| **3** typhoon | **6** flood | | **11** landslide | **14** volcanic eruption |

A. Did you hear about the _____ in ....(country)....?
B. Yes, I did. I saw it on the news.

Have you or someone you know ever experienced a natural disaster? Tell about it.

Which natural disasters sometimes happen where you live? How do people prepare for them?

## Types of Travel

1 business trip
2 family trip
3 cruise
4 (guided) tour

5 bus tour
6 train trip
7 boat trip
8 ski trip

9 study tour
10 eco-tour
11 safari
12 expedition

## Booking a Trip

13 travel agency
14 tour company
15 online
16 over the phone

[1–12]

A. Are you planning to travel soon?
B. Yes. I'm going on a _____ to ...(country)...
A. A _____ to ...(country)...? That's wonderful!

[13–16]

A. How did you make the arrangements for your trip?
B. I booked it { through a _____ [13, 14].
                _____ [15, 16].

Tell about a trip you took: Where did you travel? What kind of trip was it? How did you book the trip?

1 immigration/
   passport control
2 baggage claim area
3 customs

4 money exchange
   counter
5 taxi stand
6 shuttle bus

7 car rental counters
8 hotel courtesy
   vehicles
9 restrooms

10 passport
11 visa
12 baggage claim check
13 customs declaration form

[1–9]

A. Excuse me. { Where's ___[1, 3]___?
              { Where's the ___[2, 4–6]___?
              { Where are the ___[7–9]___?

B. Over there.

[10–13]

A. May I see your _____?
B. My _____? Yes. Here you are.
A. Thank you.

[At immigration/passport control]

A. What is the purpose of your trip—
   business or pleasure?
B. ............
A. How long do you plan to stay?
B. ............

[At customs]

A. How many bags do you have?
B. ............
A. Can you open them, please?
   I need to inspect them.
B. Certainly.

Tell about your arrival at a destination:

   Where did you arrive?
   What happened after you arrived?
   Where did you go?
   What did you do?

1 single room
2 room with double beds
3 non-smoking room
4 handicapped-accessible room
5 room with a view
6 suite

7 Room Service
8 Housekeeping
9 Maintenance
10 Front Desk
11 Concierge
12 Bell Desk

a I'd like to order *dinner*.
b We need some *towels*.
c The *sink* in our room is broken.
d I'd like a wake-up call at 7 A.M., please.
e I'd like to get tickets for *a show*.
f I'm checking out. Can you please send someone to get my bags?

[1-6]
A. I'd like a _____, please.
B. Let me see if that's available.
A. Thank you.

A. ___[7-12]___.
B. ___[a-f]___.
A. Certainly.

Tell about a hotel you stayed in: What type of room did you have? What hotel services did you use?

1 go sightseeing
2 take a walking tour
3 take a bus tour
4 exchange money

5 buy souvenirs
6 mail some postcards
7 make a restaurant reservation
8 rent a car

9 get tickets for a *show/concert*
10 visit an historic site
11 go shopping
12 go to a park

13 go to a museum
14 go to a health club/ fitness club
15 go to an Internet cafe
16 go to a club

A. May I help you?
B. Yes, please. I'd like to _____.

A. What did you do today?
B. We _____ed.

Tell about a tourist experience you had: Where did you go? What did you do there?

## Tourist Requests

## Asking Permission

## Talking with Local People

**1** exchange money

**2** cash a traveler's check

**3** buy this

**4** buy *two* tickets

**5** mail this to my country

**6** take photographs here

**7** eat here

**8** go in

**9** use a cell phone here

**10** pay with a credit card

**11** I'm from .....(country).....

**12** I'm here for *five* days.

**13** I've seen ............ and ............

**14** I like your city very much.
It's very ............

**[1–5]**

A. May I help you?

B. Yes, please. I'd like to _____.

**[6–10]**

A. Can I _____?

B. { Yes, you can.
No, you can't.

**[11–14]**

A. ___[a–d]___?

B. ___[11–14]___.

## Emergency Expressions

## Useful Expressions

15 Help!

16 Police!

17 Please don't bother me! / Please go away! /
Get away from me!

18 Fire!

19 Look out!

20 Freeze! / Stop! / Don't move!

21 Do you speak ......(language)......?

22 Please write that down for me.

23 What do you call that in English?

24 Please repeat that.

25 Please speak slowly.

26 I'm sorry. What did you say?

Be a tourist! Practice conversations with other students. Use all the expressions on pages 164 and 165.

ARCTIC
OCEAN

Baffin
Bay

GREENLAND

ICELAND

Bering
Sea

CANADA

Hudson
Bay

ALEUTIAN
ISLANDS

NORTH
AMERICA

UNITED STATES OF AMERICA

ATLANTIC
OCEAN

AZORES
(Portugal)

MOROC

CANARY ISLANDS
(Spain)

BERMUDA

HAWAIIAN ISLANDS (US)

MEXICO

Gulf of Mexico

THE BAHAMAS
CUBA

DOMINICAN
REPUBLIC
PUERTO RICO

WESTERN
SAHARA

MAURITANI

SENEGAL

CAPE VERDE

PACIFIC
OCEAN

JAMAICA
BELIZE
GUATEMALA
HONDURAS
HAITI
EL SALVADOR
NICARAGUA
COSTA RICA

VENEZUELA

GUYANA
SURINAME

GAMBIA
GUINEA-BISSAU

BL

GUINEA

SIERRA LEONE
LIBERIA

D'
GH

PANAMA
COLOMBIA

FRENCH GUIANA

LINE
ISLANDS

PHOENIX
ISLANDS

Equator

GALÁPAGOS
ISLANDS
ECUADOR

SOUTH
AMERICA

EQUAT
GUI

KIRIBATI

AMERICAN
SAMOA

MARQUESAS
ISLANDS

PERU

BRAZIL

COOK
ISLANDS

WESTERN
SAMOA

FRENCH
POLYNESIA

BOLIVIA

TONGA

TAHITI

SOCIETY
ISLANDS

PARAGUAY

AUSTRAL
ISLANDS

CHILE

N

ARGENTINA

URUGUAY

W

E

FALKLAND/MALVINAS
ISLANDS

S

Caribbean Sea

Barranquilla
Cartagena
Maracaibo
Valencia
Barquisimeto
Caracas

ATLANTIC
OCEAN

VENEZUELA

Medellín

GUYANA
Georgetown
Paramaribo
Cayenne

★ Bogotá

SURINAME    FRENCH
GUIANA

Cali

COLOMBIA

Equator                                                                    Equator

Quito

ECUADOR

Belém

Gulf of
Guayaquil
Guayaquil

Manaus

Fortaleza

Teresina

PERU

BRAZIL

Recife

Lima

Salvador

★ Brasília

La Paz

Goiânia

BOLIVIA

Sucre

Belo Horizonte

Rio de Janeiro

PARAGUAY

Campinas

CHILE

São Paulo

Asuncion

Curitiba

PACIFIC
OCEAN

Pôrto Alegre

ARGENTINA

Córdoba

Rosario

Santiago

URUGUAY

Buenos Aires

Montevideo

Gulf of San Matías

ATLANTIC
OCEAN

Gulf of
San Jorge

N

W      E

S

FALKLAND
ISLANDS

Strait of Magellan

Port Stanley

SOUTH GEORGIA
ISLAND

0          500 Miles

0        500 KM

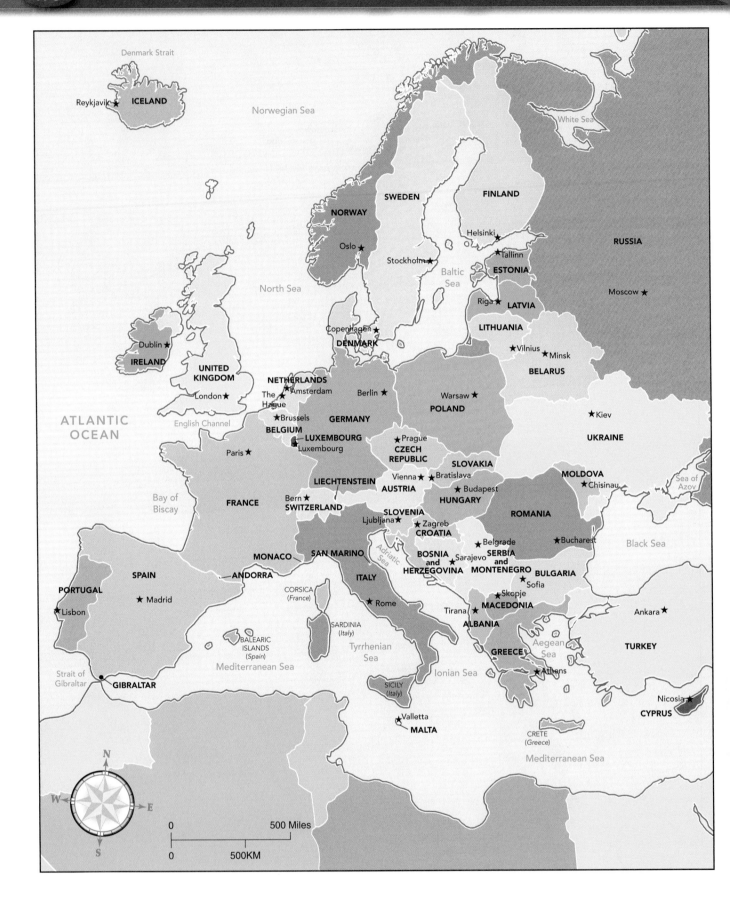

Denmark Strait

Reykjavik ★ **ICELAND**

Norwegian Sea

White Sea

**SWEDEN**

**FINLAND**

**NORWAY**

Helsinki ★

★ Tallinn

**RUSSIA**

Oslo ★

Stockholm ★

Baltic Sea

**ESTONIA**

Moscow ★

Riga ★ **LATVIA**

**LITHUANIA**

North Sea

Copenhagen ★

Vilnius ★ ★ Minsk

**DENMARK**

**BELARUS**

Dublin ★

**IRELAND**

**UNITED KINGDOM**

**NETHERLANDS**

Berlin ★

Warsaw ★

★ Kiev

London ★

★ Amsterdam
The ★
Hague

**POLAND**

ATLANTIC OCEAN

English Channel

★ Brussels

**GERMANY**

**UKRAINE**

**BELGIUM**

★ Prague

★ Prague

**LUXEMBOURG**

Luxembourg

**CZECH REPUBLIC**

Paris ★

**SLOVAKIA**

**MOLDOVA**

Vienna ★ ★ Bratislava

★ Chisinau

Sea of Azov

**LIECHTENSTEIN**

★ Budapest

**AUSTRIA**

**HUNGARY**

Bern ★

**FRANCE**

Bay of Biscay

**SWITZERLAND**

**SLOVENIA**

**ROMANIA**

Ljubljana ★

★ Zagreb

**CROATIA**

★ Bucharest

Black Sea

**MONACO**

**SAN MARINO**

Adriatic Sea

★ Belgrade

**ANDORRA**

**SERBIA and MONTENEGRO**

**BOSNIA and HERZEGOVINA**

★ Sarajevo

**BULGARIA**

**SPAIN**

**ITALY**

Sofia ★

**PORTUGAL**

★ Madrid

CORSICA (France)

★ Skopje

★ Lisbon

Rome ★

**MACEDONIA**

Ankara ★

Tirana ★

**ALBANIA**

SARDINIA (Italy)

BALEARIC ISLANDS (Spain)

Tyrrhenian Sea

**TURKEY**

Strait of Gibraltar

**GIBRALTAR**

Mediterranean Sea

Aegean Sea

**GREECE**

Ionian Sea

★ Athens

SICILY (Italy)

Nicosia ★

★ Valletta

**CYPRUS**

**MALTA**

CRETE (Greece)

Mediterranean Sea

N
W E
S

0        500 Miles

0     500KM

| Country | Nationality | Language |
|---------|-------------|----------|
| Afghanistan | Afghan | Afghan |
| Argentina | Argentine | Spanish |
| Australia | Australian | English |
| Bolivia | Bolivian | Spanish |
| Brazil | Brazilian | Portuguese |
| Bulgaria | Bulgarian | Bulgarian |
| Cambodia | Cambodian | Cambodian |
| Canada | Canadian | English/French |
| Chile | Chilean | Spanish |
| China | Chinese | Chinese |
| Colombia | Colombian | Spanish |
| Costa Rica | Costa Rican | Spanish |
| Cuba | Cuban | Spanish |
| (The) Czech Republic | Czech | Czech |
| Denmark | Danish | Danish |
| (The) Dominican Republic | Dominican | Spanish |
| Ecuador | Ecuadorian | Spanish |
| Egypt | Egyptian | Arabic |
| El Salvador | Salvadorean | Spanish |
| England | English | English |
| Estonia | Estonian | Estonian |
| Ethiopia | Ethiopian | Amharic |
| Finland | Finnish | Finnish |
| France | French | French |
| Germany | German | German |
| Greece | Greek | Greek |
| Guatemala | Guatemalan | Spanish |
| Haiti | Haitian | Haitian Kreyol |
| Honduras | Honduran | Spanish |
| Hungary | Hungarian | Hungarian |
| India | Indian | Hindi |
| Indonesia | Indonesian | Indonesian |
| Israel | Israeli | Hebrew |

| Country | Nationality | Language |
|---------|-------------|----------|
| Italy | Italian | Italian |
| Japan | Japanese | Japanese |
| Jordan | Jordanian | Arabic |
| Korea | Korean | Korean |
| Laos | Laotian | Laotian |
| Latvia | Latvian | Latvian |
| Lebanon | Lebanese | Arabic |
| Lithuania | Lithuanian | Lithuanian |
| Malaysia | Malaysian | Malay |
| Mexico | Mexican | Spanish |
| New Zealand | New Zealander | English |
| Nicaragua | Nicaraguan | Spanish |
| Norway | Norwegian | Norwegian |
| Pakistan | Pakistani | Urdu |
| Panama | Panamanian | Spanish |
| Peru | Peruvian | Spanish |
| (The) Philippines | Filipino | Tagalog |
| Poland | Polish | Polish |
| Portugal | Portuguese | Portuguese |
| Puerto Rico | Puerto Rican | Spanish |
| Romania | Romanian | Romanian |
| Russia | Russian | Russian |
| Saudi Arabia | Saudi | Arabic |
| Slovakia | Slovak | Slovak |
| Spain | Spanish | Spanish |
| Sweden | Swedish | Swedish |
| Switzerland | Swiss | German/French/Italian |
| Taiwan | Taiwanese | Chinese |
| Thailand | Thai | Thai |
| Turkey | Turkish | Turkish |
| Ukraine | Ukrainian | Ukrainian |
| (The) United States | American | English |
| Venezuela | Venezuelan | Spanish |
| Vietnam | Vietnamese | Vietnamese |

A. Where are you from?
B. I'm from **Mexico**.

A. What's your nationality?
B. I'm **Mexican**.

A. What language do you speak?
B. I speak **Spanish**.

Tell about yourself: Where are you from? What's your nationality? What languages do you speak?

Now interview and tell about a friend.

## Regular Verbs

Regular verbs have four different spelling patterns for the past and past participle forms.

**1** Add **–ed** to the end of the verb. For example:

act → act**ed**

| | | | | |
|---|---|---|---|---|
| act | cook | grill | pass | simmer |
| add | correct | guard | peel | sort |
| answer | cough | hand (in) | plant | spell |
| appear | cover | help | play | sprain |
| ask | crash | insert | polish | steam |
| assist | cross (out) | invent | pour | stow |
| attack | deliver | iron | print | stretch |
| attend | deposit | kick | reach | surf |
| bank | design | land | record | swallow |
| board | discuss | leak | register | talk |
| boil | dress | learn | relax | turn |
| box | drill | lengthen | repair | twist |
| brainstorm | dust | lift | repeat | unload |
| broil | edit | listen | request | vacuum |
| brush | end | load | respond | vomit |
| burn | enter | look | rest | walk |
| burp | establish | lower | return | wash |
| carpool | explain | mark | roast | watch |
| cash | faint | match | rock | wax |
| check | fasten | mix | saute | weed |
| clean | fix | mow | scratch | whiten |
| clear | floss | obey | seat | work |
| collect | fold | open | select | |
| comb | follow | paint | shorten | |
| construct | form | park | sign | |

**2** Add **–d** to a verb that ends in **–e**. For example:

assemble → assemble**d**

| | | | | |
|---|---|---|---|---|
| assemble | declare | grate | pronounce | shave |
| bake | describe | hire | prune | slice |
| balance | dislocate | manage | raise | sneeze |
| barbecue | dive | measure | rake | state |
| bathe | dribble | microwave | recite | style |
| bounce | enforce | move | recycle | supervise |
| browse | erase | nurse | remove | translate |
| bruise | examine | operate | revise | type |
| bubble | exchange | organize | rinse | underline |
| change | exercise | overdose | save | unscramble |
| circle | experience | practice | scrape | use |
| close | file | prepare | serve | vote |
| combine | gargle | produce | share | wheeze |

**3** Double the final consonant and add **–ed** to the end of the verb. For example:

chop → chop**ped**

| chop | mop | skip | transfer |
| hop | plan | stir | trim |
| knit | occur | stop | |

**4** Drop the final –y and add **–ied** to the end of the verb. For example:

apply → appl**ied**

| apply | dry | fry | study |
| copy | empty | stir-fry | try |

## Irregular Verbs

The following verbs have irregular past tense and/or past participle forms.

| | | | | | | |
|---|---|---|---|---|---|---|
| be | was/were | been | | know | knew | known |
| beat | beat | beaten | | leave | left | left |
| become | became | become | | let | let | let |
| bend | bent | bent | | make | made | made |
| begin | began | begun | | meet | met | met |
| bleed | bled | bled | | pay | paid | paid |
| break | broke | broken | | put | put | put |
| bring | brought | brought | | read | read | read |
| build | built | built | | rewrite | rewrote | rewritten |
| buy | bought | bought | | ring | rang | rung |
| catch | caught | caught | | run | ran | run |
| choose | chose | chosen | | say | said | said |
| come | came | come | | see | saw | seen |
| cut | cut | cut | | sell | sold | sold |
| do | did | done | | set | set | set |
| draw | drew | drawn | | shoot | shot | shot |
| drink | drank | drunk | | sing | sang | sung |
| drive | drove | driven | | sit | sat | sat |
| eat | ate | eaten | | sleep | slept | slept |
| fall | fell | fallen | | speak | spoke | spoken |
| feed | fed | fed | | stand | stood | stood |
| fly | flew | flown | | sweep | swept | swept |
| get | got | gotten | | swim | swam | swum |
| give | gave | given | | swing | swung | swung |
| go | went | gone | | take | took | taken |
| grow | grew | grown | | teach | taught | taught |
| hang | hung | hung | | throw | threw | thrown |
| have | had | had | | understand | understood | understood |
| hit | hit | hit | | withdraw | withdrew | withdrawn |
| hold | held | held | | write | wrote | written |
| hurt | hurt | hurt | | | | |

The bold number indicates the page(s) on which the word appears. The number that follows indicates the word's location in the illustration and in the word list on the page. For example, "address **1**-5" indicates that the word *address* is on page 1 and is item number 5.

## Cardinal Numbers

| | |
|---|---|
| 1 | one |
| 2 | two |
| 3 | three |
| 4 | four |
| 5 | five |
| 6 | six |
| 7 | seven |
| 8 | eight |
| 9 | nine |
| 10 | ten |
| 11 | eleven |
| 12 | twelve |
| 13 | thirteen |
| 14 | fourteen |
| 15 | fifteen |
| 16 | sixteen |
| 17 | seventeen |
| 18 | eighteen |
| 19 | nineteen |
| 20 | twenty |
| 21 | twenty-one |
| 22 | twenty-two |
| 30 | thirty |
| 40 | forty |
| 50 | fifty |
| 60 | sixty |
| 70 | seventy |
| 80 | eighty |
| 90 | ninety |
| 100 | one hundred |
| 101 | one hundred (and) one |
| 102 | one hundred (and) two |
| 1,000 | one thousand |
| 10,000 | ten thousand |
| 100,000 | one hundred thousand |
| 1,000,000 | one million |
| 1,000,000,000 | one billion |

## Ordinal Numbers

| | |
|---|---|
| 1st | first |
| 2nd | second |
| 3rd | third |
| 4th | fourth |
| 5th | fifth |
| 6th | sixth |
| 7th | seventh |
| 8th | eighth |
| 9th | ninth |
| 10th | tenth |
| 11th | eleventh |
| 12th | twelfth |
| 13th | thirteenth |
| 14th | fourteenth |
| 15th | fifteenth |
| 16th | sixteenth |
| 17th | seventeenth |
| 18th | eighteenth |
| 19th | nineteenth |
| 20th | twentieth |
| 21st | twenty-first |
| 22nd | twenty-second |
| 30th | thirtieth |
| 40th | fortieth |
| 50th | fiftieth |
| 60th | sixtieth |
| 70th | seventieth |
| 80th | eightieth |
| 90th | ninetieth |
| 100th | one hundredth |
| 101st | one hundred (and) first |
| 102nd | one hundred (and) second |
| 1,000th | one thousandth |
| 10,000th | ten thousandth |
| 100,000th | one hundred thousandth |
| 1,000,000th | one millionth |
| 1,000,000,000th | one billionth |

## Days of the Week

Sunday
Monday
Tuesday
Wednesday
Thursday
Friday
Saturday

## Months of the Year

| | |
|---|---|
| January | July |
| February | August |
| March | September |
| April | October |
| May | November |
| June | December |